C000094270

Threads of Hope

Threads of Hope:

Counselling and Emotional Support Services for Communities in Crisis

A narrative inquiry reflecting on the Listening Point project in Machynlleth following the murder of April Jones

With Anne Marie, Ceri, Hope, Lisa, Maria, and other volunteers from Listening Point

By

Susan Dale

Cambridge Scholars Publishing

Threads of Hope:
Counselling and Emotional Support Services for Communities in Crisis

By Susan Dale

This book first published 2016

Cambridge Scholars Publishing

Lady Stephenson Library, Newcastle upon Tyne, NE6 2PA, UK

British Library Cataloguing in Publication Data
A catalogue record for this book is available from the British Library

ISBN (10): 1-4438-8732-3
ISBN (13): 978-1-4438-8732-8

This book is dedicated to the people of Machynlleth, and surrounding villages, who have been a beacon of inspiration in a very dark place.

TABLE OF CONTENTS

ACKNOWLEDGEMENTS

It takes a team of committed people to run a project such as Listening Point, and a team to produce a book such as this one. Although I took the lead on managing the project, and have been the lead author and editor for this publication, it has been a team effort. I could not have done either task without the support, encouragement and input from the volunteers who have given so much of their time, skill and compassion. I am so very glad to have met them, and to call them my friends.

With respect to starting and running the project, so many people from the local community and beyond gave so much support and energy that it would be difficult to include all of them. Some of those whom I particularly want to thank are: the Police Family Liaison Officers Dave and Hayley; Kath Rogers, Priest in Charge of St Peter's Church, and elders from other local churches who offered venues and undertook fundraising; the Welsh Presbyterian Church, who also donated towards the start-up costs; counselling colleagues, including Liz Loyd, based just outside Machynlleth, Jane and Elyan, practitioners based in nearby Twyn, Jan Hillman, my clinical supervisor, and Hugh Fox, who provided a narrative therapy perspective; other community leaders such as Mike Williams, local and district counsellor, and the mayor and town council of Machynlleth, who provided help and support throughout the life of the project; Powys Council, for granting the lease of the building; Andrew, the Bishop of Bangor, who ensured funds were found in respect of the start-up costs; my fellow trustees of the Churches Counselling Service in Wales, who supported and gave an infrastructure to the project; my fellow Iona Community members, who gave funds, support, prayer and practical advice when needed; Paul and Coral, April's parents, who, despite their own terrible loss, encouraged the project to get off the ground; Cruse, who provided the initial training for volunteers; local schools, who distributed flyers and encouraged families to access the services, and companies such as Next, Mid Wales Co-op and local shops, who donated products ranging from cushions and throws to tea bags.

There was also the generosity of people within the local communities who brought cakes, flowers, plants and jigsaws, and visitors from across the world who also brought good wishes and sometimes donations. The level of support from so many was truly humbling.

The writing of the book has also needed the additional skills of a publisher willing to publish, colleagues, including Kim Etherington, Catherine Jackson and Paidraig Ó Tuama, who have given supervision feedback on the text and encouragement when I have been flagging. Finally, I would not have achieved any of this without the patience, love and support of my family, especially John, who have accompanied me through both the project and the writing about it.

Prologue

"Among the darkness of the night a small act of kindness seems like a small silver thread of hope reaching out across the abyss."
—Anon

The last week of September 2012 was nothing out of the ordinary for me: the usual round of appointments with clients in my consulting room in the centre of Machynlleth, followed by the wave of counselling supervisees coming to my garden study at home. This, together with my editing work for a counselling journal, was my normal working life: a mix that I have always enjoyed and felt privileged to do. Sunday had been a day of quiet celebration with my husband John: it was his birthday. Although my physical health had not been brilliant, the year had been a relatively good one, with writing, work and family in balance.

We were preparing for bed when there was a knock at the back door. John answered it:

"A little girl has gone missing off the Bryn-y-Gog; they think she has got into a light-coloured van," a man's voice says. "She's only five. Have you seen anything?"

I have, of course, seen nothing: I am vision impaired and have no night vision. I have seen nothing, but I imagine everything. A little girl of five, out there in the black night, while I am here, in the warm of my home, frozen in bed; useless.

Frozen, I lie there.
No feelings; numb, dumb silence.

I wake to light flashing through the darkness, the silence pierced by the vibrations of the passing helicopter.
"Where are you April?"

Terror creeps through the windows.
This was a safe place;

the unseen hills close in.
I find it difficult to breathe.

The morning brings a new day, a parallel universe that has opened up all around me. In the field at the bottom my garden are teams of people searching, rain pouring down their faces. Silence is broken by an anguished, "It's time to come home now, April." The television is on for the breakfast news and I see my own garden. I still feel frozen. "I should, I could," I think, but what I need to do I do not know.

There is dread: knowledge that something is unfolding here that is terrible and world changing beyond belief.

INTRODUCTION

Format and map through the book

This book uses a narrative research methodology to tell the story of one group of people who were involved as volunteers in a project called Listening Point, which was set up to support the community of Machynlleth following the abduction of five-year-old April Jones on 1st October 2012. It aims to capture our experiences of living in and around Machynlleth along a time-line starting from the day that April was abducted through to September 2014 when the Listening Point project came to an end.

This introduction will offer some brief background information about the events in Machynlleth between October 2012 and October 2013, and an introduction to the narrative research methodology used to inform the book.

The book is a collaborative effort. Each chapter begins with an excerpt from my ethnographic journal and quotes from press releases released at that time, and then interweaves theory with the narratives provided by my co-researchers.

It also offers our conclusions and considerations, based on what we learned from our experiences in Machynlleth, for those contemplating setting up services for communities during times of crisis, and an appendix with statistics gathered over the course of the project.

The research seeks to look at the particular moments in our lives. It is, for that reason, deliberately subjective and, because as psychotherapeutic practitioners we are interested in thoughts, feelings and behaviours, it teases out our personal responses to this traumatic event by sharing our thoughts from those times and reflecting on them from where we are today.

The research is dynamic, changing even as we wrote; it will never be a "finished story" but always, for us, a work in progress. Every telling evokes in us a different response, and the narrative gets "thicker and richer" (White 2007a). We tell the emotive stories not to elicit sympathy but because they document an implicit (White 1999) story of hope, human endeavour, and of one group of people for whom children, family and community are deeply precious.

Summary of events

On 1st October 2012 five-year-old April Jones was abducted from the Bryn-y-Gog estate in Machynlleth, where she lived with her parents and two older siblings. Her disappearance triggered Dyfed Powys police force to launch the UK's largest ever search operation of its kind and an investigation that lasted over six months. The search effort covered gardens, fields, farms, outbuildings and septic tanks, and a systematic, fingertip search covering a 15 mile radius around Machynlleth – rugged terrain that included forest, mountain, moor, rivers, a river estuary and coastline. It was anticipated that it would cost between £1.8 and £2.4 million (it is thought the final cost far exceeded this, but final figures have not been released).

Machynlleth is a market town of just 2,000 inhabitants, situated in remote Powys, on the edge of Snowdonia National Park. It is surrounded by rugged mountain terrain, managed forests, rivers, disused slate quarries and hills grazed by sheep. The river Dyfi (Dovey) runs down into the estuary and sea at the nearby coastal village of Aberdovey. The two largest nearest towns are Aberystwyth, a university town with 13,000 inhabitants, 18 miles away, and Newtown, 29 miles distant, with a population of 19,500.

On average, every day for six months 150 professionals were out searching for April. They included police and mountain rescue teams, divers, forensic officers and dog handlers from all over the UK, as well as coastguards, RNLI officers, local police community and family liaison officers, and administration and catering teams, who all had to be accommodated in local coastal hotels. A temporary police command centre was set up, first in the local leisure centre; then, as it became obvious the search effort would take many weeks, in one of the business units on the edge of Machynlleth. Police, search and rescue helicopters regularly landed in the school playing field.

Added to the professionals were the hundreds of civilian volunteers from all over the UK, who also needed hotel accommodation, and the media – film crews and reporters, who descended on the town from all over the world.

It may help readers to follow the rest of the narrative if I list the key dates here.

- 1st October 2012 – Hundreds of local volunteers join the search for April, which goes on through the night.
- 2nd October 2012 – Mark Bridger, a local man, whose children attend the same school as April, is arrested, accused of abducting April. The search continues, police working alongside volunteers who have been arriving from all over the UK.
- 5th October 2012 – April has still not been found, but Mark Bridger appears before magistrates charged with her abduction and murder. The professional search effort continues, but local volunteers are stood down.
- 7th October 2012 – Over 700 people walk from the Bryn-y-Gog Estate to St Peter's Church in Machynlleth, where a service is held for April.
- November 2012 – The Listening Point project is launched to support the community in Machynlleth. Twelve volunteer listeners are recruited and trained.
- 20 December 2012 – Listening Point opens a drop-in centre at St Peter's Church office in the centre of Machynlleth.
- 14th January 2013 – Mark Bridger appears in Mold Crown Court and denies all charges, but his barrister states that he "recognised he was probably responsible for her death" (BBC News).
- 25th February 2013 – Mark Bridger appears in Mold Crown Court, and the trial is adjourned.
- 26th September 2013 – Hundreds of people line the streets and attend April's funeral at St Peter's Church in Machynlleth.

- 27th March 2014 – Dyfed Powys Police announce that the search efforts will be scaled back by the end of April.

- 24th April 2014 – Listening Point moves from St Peter's Church office to a new centre on the Bryn-y-Gog estate. The drop-in service is supplemented by the start of a confidential counselling service and creative workshops for families.

- 29th April 2014 – Mark Bridger's trial starts at Mold Crown Court. April's parents attend.

- 30th May 2014 – The jury unanimously finds Mark Bridger guilty of abducting and murdering April and of perverting the course of justice, after just over four hours of deliberation. On sentencing him to a whole life term in prison, the judge calls him a "pathological liar" and "a paedophile" (BBC News).

- 28th September 2014 – the Listening Point project closes, having offered telephone and drop-in support and comfort to nearly 650 people and more formal counselling to another 32.

Narrative Research: Methodological Considerations

"What is the purpose of all these stories? What can they hope to achieve? They cannot change what happened to April?" I am mindful of my inner critic, and also of the academic quest for "truth" and an "evidence base". Narrative inquiry can never hope to find the "truth" about what happened to April, or the "truth" about Machynlleth, or even what Listening Point meant to those involved with it. Narrative inquiry can, however, look for the "talk that sings" (Bird 2004, 61) – the stories that bring to life a world others cannot imagine. It can give a unique glimpse into the lived experience of a particular group of people engaged at a particular moment in time and in a particular place in the shared task of trying to support themselves and their small community through the abduction and murder of a small child, a major police search and investigation, the trial and conviction of a local man for the death, all under the intense scrutiny of the world media.

This research is presented as a collaborative narrative inquiry that explores the experience of setting up and running a project to support the local community following the abduction and murder of April Jones. It is deliberately and overtly subjective. It takes an "up close and personal" (Bird 2000) look at our (my own and that of my co-researchers) experiences of this unique event. This narrative inquiry embraces many strands of methodological practice. It is ethnographic – in the Oxford English dictionary definition of "the systematic study of people and cultures". As the Association for Quantitative Research points out, ethnography originates from anthropology, which

> … traditionally refers to a practice in which researchers spend long periods living within a culture in order to study it. The term has been adopted within qualitative market research to describe occasions where researchers spend time–hours, days or weeks–observing and/or interacting with participants in areas of their everyday lives (http://www.aqr.org.uk/glossary/ethnography).

Researching and documenting situations and people's responses to them when those people are in difficult or challenging situations is fraught with ethical challenges. A question I have asked myself is: should we try to document this project within this particular community at a time of tragedy? Behar (1997, 2) answers with another question, one that resonates for the co-researchers and me: "But if you can't stop the horror, shouldn't you at least document it?"

Behar describes the task of anthropology as one of really understanding people within a specific culture and time and as a task that needs to break your heart or it is worth nothing. These words also resonate deeply with me in relation to my own experiences in Machynlleth. She writes:

> The desire to enter into the world around you and having no idea how to do it, the fear of observing too coldly or too distractedly or too raggedly, the rage of cowardice, the insight that is always arriving late, as defiant hindsight, a sense of the utter uselessness of writing anything and yet the burning desire to write something are the stopping places along the way (Behar 1999, 1).

This research is also auto-ethnographic in part, in that it uses my own reflections from that time and from the present day to offer an understanding of life during that time and within that specific culture. It is also partly a collective biography. It draws, to borrow from Speedy,

> … upon the early memory work of Haug (1987) in its form of drawing together a group of 'biographers' to share memories of common experience

> and through talking and writing develop a 'collective biography' which produces a 'web' of experiences that are at once individual, connected collective (Speedy and Wyatt, 2014a, 52; also Davies and Gannon 2006).

We have written this to inform other communities who find themselves in similar situations, in the hope that it may help them anticipate some of the challenges and devise their own creative solutions.

Our hope is also that our narratives will be some help to social science researchers who are interested in the effects of trauma on communities, and those using both narrative research and narrative therapy to provide therapeutic interventions.

The process of research itself may be part of the unfolding narrative, and may add another layer to a "multi-layered narrative" (Banks 1998) of the events under scrutiny.

We have experienced the process of writing and constructing the narratives as "the final part" and "ending" of the Listening Point project. It has enabled us to think through what we did well, and what we wished we had done better. It has also, as one of the volunteers commented, "helped us process the trauma we experienced during this time". We did not set out specifically with a therapeutic goal, but the research and writing has proved therapeutic for us. We have documented it as best we can, using ourselves as both the researchers and the research subjects in order that others in similar situations may learn from our experiences. (Further details of the use of narrative inquiry as a tool for research are given in Chapter four.)

We have tried very hard to only share our own stories, and not to invade the privacy, or to make comment on, what other people (those not involved in the writing) thought or felt at the time. We have written it with the knowledge of April's family, who have been inspiring and who have supported all we have done through Listening Point, despite their overwhelming personal grief.

Presentation of the Text

It would be wrong to write a multi-layered, dynamic narrative such as this using academic language. You will find here a range of voices and styles of writing, each presented in a different typeface or font to clarify the difference. You will find the narrative text, in this serif type face; my informal journal entries, in *italic font*; rescued speech poems (Behan, 2003) taken from conversations with the co-researchers and informal writing from contributors, both in a sans serif typeface, and also quotes from other research and academics, which are indented from the main text and in a smaller font, as is traditional in academic publishing. By presenting the text in this way we aim to give the same value and weight to personal accounts that is generally accorded to more academic writing.

We also hope the text presentation will help readers to appreciate the "texture" and "weave" created by of so many different voices contributing to the narrative.

Introducing the Co-researchers and Contributors

Listening Point would not have existed without the expertise, skill and dedication of the team of volunteer listeners, counsellors and others who cheered us on from the sidelines. The writing of the book has been a collaborative effort. I, as author, have acted as editor and had the task of weaving the threads of story together to form a coherent narrative.

All people co-researching and contributing to this book have chosen to do so; some have had the time to contribute much, others just a snippet here and there, but all of these contributions are valuable and make up the whole (which is always greater than the parts alone). Contributors have chosen whether to remain anonymous or to write in their own names, and sometimes to withdraw, or edit material. Some of those who have written under their own names have included a short biography; others have chosen not to. We have tried very hard not to presume we understand how anyone else might feel about the events we describe, and to respect the privacy of those around us.

My work in research, writing and therapeutic work is underpinned by the BACP Ethical Framework for the Counselling Professions. You can find a copy of this document at www.bacp.co.uk/ethicalframework. You can find more in chapter 14 about the complex ethical challenges posed by the project.

Named contributors (alphabetical)

Anne Marie Carty

Anne Marie is a film-maker and visual ethnographer specialising in the use of video as a tool for engagement in Welsh rural communities. She has lived in Machynlleth since 1995 and has recently been exploring the use of narrative therapy approaches in participatory film-making and co-research with young people and adults.

Ceri Edwards

Ceridwen Edwards is a retired homoeopath, counsellor and alternative health therapist, and the mother of five sons.

Hope Marshall

Hope is a counsellor working in the Machynlleth area with a background in mental health nursing. She was born in Shropshire but has enjoyed living in Wales for many years. She is happily married with grown-up children and one grandchild, who lives in America.

June

Lisa Lovatt-Sutton

Lisa lives with her husband and two dogs in beautiful Mid Wales. Originally from Leicestershire, she moved to Wales in 2012. She is blessed with an amazing family and will become a Grandma for the first time this year.

Her background is in the health sector, combining hypnotherapy and counselling and, since coming to Wales, she has enjoyed voluntary work in the community.

Liz

Mark

Maria Morris

Melanie Fraser

Melanie has lived in Mid Wales for nearly 30 years, with her husband and their son (who has now flown the nest). Recently training as a counsellor, she now works in what she considers her “dream job” as a Children's Counsellor.

Melody

Sue Winchurch

Sue is an experienced counsellor living and working in and around Machynlleth. She specialises in working with adult survivors of childhood sexual abuse and clients with drug and alcohol issues. In addition, Sue takes on a number of Private Clients from Powys and Ceredigion.

Other contributors include Powys Cruse and other volunteers and visitors to Listening Point

Chapter One

Searching for April

Sue's journal: 2nd October 2012

A knock on the door yesterday evening brought an end to peace, and brought with it a night of dread. A story of a child missing from the Bryn-y-Gog estate; seen getting into a grey van/car. People out searching all night, calling April's name in the vast black wilderness and woodland that surrounds our town.

08:00 BBC Breakfast News is relayed from the end of our drive. The rain is relentless, the searchers drenched, weeping, calling for April as they comb gardens, sheds and farmers' fields. An elderly man shouts at them, "What are you doing?" He has not heard the news. It is hard to believe. I hand a young woman a mug of tea as she comes into the garden. She sobs: "If we just keep looking we will find her."

09:00 I am due to meet with clients in my consulting rooms in the middle of town. Not knowing what else to do, I walk there. Above I can hear the sound of helicopters; a sound I will get to know very well over the months ahead. There are numerous police; people handing out flyers to anyone passing: "Have you seen this child?" – enormous energy, doing something; anything is better than doing nothing. An elderly woman weeps in the bus queue: "I am too old to be useful," she says.

My clients arrive, traumatised; most unable to bring themselves to speak of themselves. All thoughts are of the young girl missing, out there in the wild wet hillside, somewhere.

12:00 The weather (still torrential rain) and a news update give no further relief. More police arrive, including mountain rescue and dog teams. The volunteers are being organised into teams. More arrive, some with food and drink for those going out. The rain still falls like razors to the ground. The press start to talk about "unprecedented community support". I wonder what will happen when we have to stop "doing". Then I feel guilty: this thought feels like a betrayal of hope.

Reverend Kathleen Rogers is interviewed, along with members of the local council. The message is clear: "We will not give up hope: we will not give up looking for April."

18:00 A local man has been arrested on grounds of abduction, but still the police search continues. The river is full of divers. April's parents make an appeal to "let our beautiful little girl come home". The shock of the arrest, together with the ongoing search, leaves me feeling bewildered. What are the police saying? April has been murdered, or April is lost?

Volunteers are still involved, but in my heart I know that they will soon be stood down. I cannot even voice my deepest fear; I know that this is turning into an investigation for those with forensic skills, but to say so would be like giving up on the hope that keeps everyone going.

22:00 Still the helicopters fly overhead, their searchlights brightening the sky.

Waking later in the night, there is a new silence. This feels even more ominous and I find myself drenched in sweat.

Community update

2nd October 2012
08:00 "The breaking news this morning comes live from the small Mid Wales market town of Machynlleth where hundreds of local people and police teams have been out all night searching for the missing schoolgirl, April Jones. April, aged five, who is thought to have been abducted, went missing whilst playing with friends close to her home in Machynlleth yesterday evening. The search operation is being co-ordinated from the local leisure centre by Dyfed Powys Police." (BBC Breakfast)

Trauma

All of us at some time during our lives will experience situations that we find traumatic – situations that shock us or challenge everything we thought we knew to be true. We need the resilience (Skodol 2010), and opportunity, to find the internal resources and strategies to continue to live our lives and integrate this new knowledge. Most of the time we adapt very well and the events that proved traumatic become stepping stones along our life journey, sometimes even enabling our development. An example of this was given by Mark, who attended a "trauma" workshop that I recently facilitated. He spoke about arriving at university for first time:

> My parents brought my cases in and then they left me there in my little cell. I was surrounded by a hoard of people I didn't know and, as a shy boy, this felt like the end of the world. I remember shaking and crying. However, it was, I think, the making of me. I had to re-think who I was. I could choose to stay in my room and speak to no one, or I could go out there and act in a different way. I did, and I found I really enjoyed it.
>
> Although it felt very traumatic at the time, and I had anxiety attacks and could not sleep, it helped me become who I am now. Without it, I would probably have lived at home with Mum forever. It has become like a piece of my history now; I remember the pain, but it is no longer painful.

However, some experiences are so traumatic that we cannot transform the memory into a format that fits in with our view of the world, our belief systems and our other relationships and experiences. These traumatic memories are not filed away as historic memories with context; they remain isolated pockets of emotional pain and fear, and physical and sensory response. When we are triggered by particular circumstances or sensory stimuli, we may experience pain and/or distress, not in relation to a memory of a historical event long past, but as something horrific happening in the here and now. For example, the smell of honeysuckle reminds me of being a child in rural Suffolk, where I played in the garden as a small child. The memory runs in my mind, a bit like an old film, fitting neatly between other events. If, however, I had experienced a traumatic event that linked with the smell of honeysuckle (for example, childhood abuse) then that smell might instead evoke the pain and anguish that accompanied the original event. I might experience vivid flashbacks of the event, or even relive the terror. Or I might experience extreme physical or emotional pain and not know what has caused it. As the symptoms I experience are not embedded in a historic past, or even linked with what is going on around me, these feelings could be experienced as more painful than the event itself.

For example, Liz tells me of her experience of flashbacks:

> I was standing in the queue at Tesco. There was a man in front of me; I could smell his aftershave, a spicy, quite pleasant smell. I suddenly felt really hot and panicky. My breath started coming in short bursts; I felt unreasonably terrified. I thought I might wet myself... I just pushed the trolley back into supermarket and went outside. I thought I was going to die, or go mad.

Later Liz realised that the aftershave smelled like the one her father used; he had sexually abused her for many years.

Other people have described post-traumatic symptoms in terms of “being haunted”, “torture” or even “a never-ending hell of replaying the event”.

We have a tendency to think that “trauma” is a new condition but it has been described in many different ways and given many different names over our history. Fussell quotes Siegfried Sassoon describing the return of soldiers from World War I:

> Shell shock. How many a brief bombardment had its long-delayed after-effect in the minds of these survivors. Not then was their evil hour, but now; now, in the sweating suffocation of nightmare, in paralysis of limbs, in the stammering of dislocated speech. In the name of civilisation these soldiers had been martyred, and it remained for civilisation to prove that their martyrdom wasn’t a dirty swindle (Fussell 1983, 141).

Not everyone who is exposed to trauma goes on to develop permanent trauma symptoms or post-traumatic stress disorder (PTSD) (Bonanno 2004), or have the same responses to a traumatic event (Terr 1991). Certainly there are many in Machynlleth who would not consider that they have been traumatised or that they have any trauma symptoms. This may be because their prior life experiences, resilience or any number of factors mean that they have been able to process the memory of April's abduction as a historic event, albeit a sad one.

One elderly lady visiting the drop-in tells me:

> These things happen. They are terrible things, but you just have to get on with living and clinging on to all that is good. Other bad things have happened here, and they have passed. So will this.

For others, however, the events have left invisible scars. For example, one of the volunteers reported feelings of panic and extreme anxiety while away on holiday when she encountered a television crew filming a routine event in London. Local children seemed to become unusually (for children) unwilling to be photographed with visiting celebrities at carnival events, and tended to disappear from view at the sight of reporters or TV cameras.

In hindsight I realise that I too was traumatised and "frozen" by the unfolding events. As an experienced therapist, I was surprised by this. My journal captures something of this dual role: I was supporting clients and supervisees, and yet I was also a member of our community.

Therapeutic approaches to community trauma

There are many ways of responding to individuals or groups of people affected by trauma; not all are necessarily a professional intervention. When what the police describe as a "critical incident" occurs, we are often able, during or soon after the event, to process our thoughts and feelings about it, so that we can engage again with normal life.

Talking to our friends and families can be sufficient; sometimes, if it is an event that affects a whole community, coming together with others also affected can help "normalise" and "put into perspective" our thoughts and fears. For example, in 2011 the threat of a dam bursting meant a small neighbouring village had to be evacuated. Some residents described having to flee their homes as "traumatic". They met in the local leisure centre. Talking and encouraging one another turned an alarming experience into one that they could encounter together. The trauma had engendered "a war-time spirit", as one man said. Later that night, when the crisis had been averted, they were allowed home. A few reported having nightmares about "what *might* have happened", but the majority considered it "just another saga in the life of a Welsh village" (elderly resident).

The same leisure centre was used on the night that April went missing. People gathered together, supporting and encouraging another as they searched for her through the night. The next day they searched again, handed out flyers, talked to each other, and made tea and sandwiches for the many visiting police teams.

What happens if the traumatic event continues over a long period of time or escalates and people are unable to meet together for support? Or if the traumatic events trigger overwhelming emotional responses relating to people's own unprocessed feelings, memories and relationships? For example, in the months following April's murder I received many calls on the telephone helpline from people who reported that the news had triggered memories of their own childhood abuse, or the death of a loved one; some reported suicidal thoughts and one described vivid memories of another child who went missing some 60 years previously.

In Machynlleth we seemed to be under continual assault from new and shocking facts as they emerged through the media and police reports. The intense media attention meant we felt under constant scrutiny. Each new factor added another layer of tension and trauma in a location that is geographically cut off from the outside world – the nearest large town, Aberystwyth, is more than 18 miles away. One resident told me he was taking the train to Birmingham once a week "just so I can be anonymous".

Sometimes a traumatic event that happens within a community coincides with a trauma in our own lives, and the two traumas, which individually we might have been able to take in our stride, become jumbled together. Ceri writes to me:

> I will always remember that day, that week. I have a slow motion recollection of it, with heightened senses around the memory because of the extremes of emotion. I had been so happy, celebrating a special birthday, and had been away for the weekend then back to Machynlleth and the rain – wondering, would we be able to get across the bridge to drive to the restaurant that we were supposed to be meeting friends at for a quiet meal?

The river was very high but we made it, and I had the added surprise of not just a few friends but a big surprise party, all organised for me in total secrecy. The next day I was relaxed and happy and didn't see or hear the news, and I don't do social media, so it was the day after when I had a doctor's appointment that I first heard from the local GP, who told me that April had been abducted: "Such a terrible thing to happen here, I don't know how could such a thing happen in a place like this." Of course nobody knew at that time that April was dead.

My lodgers came home at mid-day saying everyone up at CAT [the Centre for Alternative Technology] had decided to join the search as they couldn't concentrate on work. I still felt optimistic and thought there must be some sort of mistake and it would all turn out well. Of course we soon knew that it really wasn't going to turn out well.

By the following weekend the town was full of people searching and there was a police presence everywhere, with the search concentrated on the bridge and the river, which is very close to my house. We went out but my partner was taken ill suddenly and we came home and rang the hospital for guidance. They said we must call an ambulance – he had had a heart attack.

Everything seemed totally surreal.

Community, religion and trauma

Van der Kolk, McFarlane and Weisaeth comment that:

> … people have always gathered in communities and organisations for aid in dealing with outside challenges. They seek close emotional relationships with others in order to help them anticipate, meet, and integrate difficult experiences (van der Kolk, Mc Farlane, and Weisaeth 1996, 24).

They go on to argue that, in western European culture, traditions and value systems have been historically provided by Christian communities, with the Church "often providing a sense of purpose in the face of terrifying realities" (ibid, 24).

In the UK, however, the Church no longer plays a large part in many people's lives. Some are even distrustful of and avoid formal religions. Many areas of the UK are now multicultural, embracing many religions and secularism. In Machynlleth the population is predominantly white with a mixture of Welsh-speaking Welsh, English-speaking Welsh, and English, and a small number of people from other ethnic groups. There are no mosques, synagogues or temples, but there are five churches: St Peter's (Church in Wales), Machynlleth Community Church, St Mair (Catholic Church) and two Welsh Chapels. These mainly have small older congregations, as do the churches in the surrounding villages. Although the churches in Machynlleth try to support one another, historically throughout Wales there have often been divisions between the different denominations – divisions of language (Welsh versus English) and differences in style of worship.

Yet on the Sunday following April's abduction hundreds of people walked to St Peter's and joined in the service of worship. The same happened at April's funeral the following September.

Throughout this time St Peter's remained open in daylight hours and many local people and searchers sought its quiet space and lit candles there in memory of April. A memorial book in the side chapel contains thousands of entries written by people from across the world:

> God Bless you little April, I cry for you every night. I hope and pray you rest in peace. (Melody, a visitor from US)

However attendance at regular services has not changed and still remains low.

Listening Point was originally based in a building that also houses the church office and meeting room. Some visitors reported feeling uncomfortable about coming there; one man firmly told me, "I don't want to talk to church do-gooders." When we moved to the Bryn-y-Gog Estate people seemed to find it easier to drop in, even though we were the same group of people – some regular church goers, others of different faiths or none at all.

Secondary trauma

The trauma of the unfolding story affected not just April's family and the inhabitants of Machynlleth. Other people across the world and the media who covered the story were witnessing the events through the television, radio, camera lens or newspaper.

Symptoms of trauma are not just experienced by those who are immediately involved in tragedy or abuse; they can also affect those who support them or are witness to the horror of the story. Berthold describes this as "trauma [which] involves a transformation of the helper's inner experience, resulting from empathic engagement with client's trauma material" (Berthold 2014).

A young reporter, herself in tears, asked me: "Why are so many people so devastated by the murder of this young girl. Yes, it is sad, but it is as if they have lost their own children."

I could not answer her then, or explain the paradox of her question, accompanied as it was by her tears. I am not sure I can answer it now, but for many of us April seemed like our child too. It wasn't that we imagined ourselves to feel as April's parents did, but perhaps we felt we were standing alongside them, empathising with and attuned to their loss, and this combined with our own fear of losing our loved ones and even, perhaps, our own histories of parenthood and loss.

The growing press coverage and the reporting of the story as it unfolded provoked reactions even in those who lived hundreds of miles away. Van der Kolk and colleagues suggest:

> The personal meaning of traumatic experience for individuals is influenced by the social context in which it occurs. Victims and the significant people in their surroundings may have different and fluctuating assessments of both the reality of what has happened and of the extent of the victims' suffering. As a result, victims and bystanders may have strongly conflicting agendas to repair, create, forget or take revenge. These conflicts between the victims' and the bystanders' assessment of the meaning of the trauma may set the stage for the trauma to be perpetuated in a larger social setting; soon the allocation of blame and responsibility, not the trauma itself, may become the central issue (van der Kolk, McFarlane and Weisaeth 1996, 27).

Perhaps April's disappearance and death were experienced as traumatic within our community because of our compassion for her family; the resonances with our own losses, and the plague of media who invaded our town with their intrusive cameras and microphones. Perhaps, too, it was our shock and fear that something so terrible had happened in a place we considered "safe", a place we thought we knew. In those moments there were, perhaps, assumptions of shared identity.

The search effort

The statistics about Machynlleth, as reported on the BBC News website in October 2012, show the extent to which the community was flooded with outsiders in those early weeks. In addition to our population of 2,000 residents, there were:

- 200 police, divers, RNLI and mountain rescue teams from all over the UK deployed on the search within a five-mile radius of the town centre
- 400 local volunteers assisting with the search and based at the leisure centre until they were "stood down" at the end of the first week
- 20 local volunteers assisting with cooking and washing up for the search teams on a regular basis from a temporary port-a-cabin in the grounds of the council offices (this continued for three months, until a professional catering service was provided)
- three helicopter teams helping with the search, and additional helicopters sent by national media teams.

One thousand people attended the church service in Machynlleth on that first Sunday.

The professional in me kept expecting that "someone" would set up some kind of support service for the wider community and the burgeoning numbers of visitors, but the days turned into a week and still nothing had happened. As the search became more professional and the volunteers were stood down, I noticed a change in me and in those around me:

Sue's journal: 8th October 2012

The energy of the last few days has gone. Whereas last week people were rushing about trying to do something, anything to find April, now there is an eerie silence in the town. People walk about with their heads down, not making eye contact with anyone. Shopping is done out of necessity; no frivolity, no laughing, just rain and silence. Police can be seen in the surrounding hills and river, scouring the ground and wading in the cold black water.

I am starting to emerge from my "frozen" state, and am beginning to think again like a therapist! I think now I know what I need to do.

I started consciously to assess what resources Machynlleth had in terms of psychological support.

At that time Machynlleth had one GP practice with three doctors in the town centre, and another small surgery with two GPs five miles away in a neighbouring village. The mental health services in Powys (a large county) are stretched, with patients sometimes waiting for up to 24 months for psychiatric or psychological assessments. There were at the time no emergency mental health beds in the county.

I have been told by one of the local GPs that there is a higher than average incidence of serious mental health disorders in Machynlleth. There is also a long waiting list for referrals to the community mental health team and the child and adolescent mental health service (CAMHS) serving the area.

People could be referred for counselling by their GP, and to the specialist substance misuse services, and for some online, CBT-based self-help programmes. In addition at the time there were a very few experienced counsellors and psychotherapists working privately in the area. I was the only BACP accredited (British Association of Counselling and Psychotherapy) practitioner working in the town, and I also supervised many of the trainees and less experienced practitioners who worked locally.

However, people in Machynlleth tended not to make much use of counselling. Some of the referrals to my private practice were people who lived locally, but many more came from the surrounding towns and villages, or were referred by other bodies such as employee assistance providers, local authority children's services, social workers and local employers. The cultural norm for those who had grown up in the area seemed to be, as one person told me, "We don't usually talk to outsiders about personal stuff."

Following April's abduction, Powys Health Board provided funding for a professional counsellor in Newtown (some 30 miles away) to offer people sessions, but this service did not appear to be used and was not widely advertised. The primary school received support from the local branch of the bereavement support charity Cruse, and Cruse and also later helped Listening Point by providing initial listening skills training to volunteers and by taking referrals for counselling. A voluntary sector counselling service also increased the number of sessions it provided at the local secondary school. April's siblings and Mark Bridger's children attended the same local schools, which had to be handled with great sensitivity.

But beyond these, there was no organised source of emotional or psychological support for the people of Machynlleth – or none that they felt able easily to access.

In the month following April's disappearance the police welfare officer and chaplain were providing assistance to the police search teams and the local volunteers. However, once the local volunteers were disbanded and professional forensic specialists arrived to conduct the murder investigation, the police did not have enough resources to support the local community.

It became clear to me that we needed to organise our own community support, and that I might be best placed to lead it. There were drawbacks in that I lived in the community and was also affected by the issues. Ethically, too, there were potential problems if I were to hold dual roles as senior practitioner and project lead. The advantages, however, were that I already had an intimate knowledge of the community, and had managed similar community projects before. I spoke at length to colleagues and to my own counselling supervisor – their wisdom and expertise would enable me to work safely, both in terms of my therapeutic work with clients and in guarding me from burn-out. If I did take the lead, I would need to put in place suitable supervision and a robust personal support system to be able to engage with the task.

I then began to think about what kind of service might be needed, how best to introduce it, and who I would need to work with – the police teams and community leaders, the local GPs, churches and other voluntary groups – to ensure they were supportive of any proposed plans. I would also need to research the resources that already existed and could be tapped into. CAMAD (Community Action Machynlleth and District), for example, was extremely helpful in suggesting both venues and ways of approaching potential volunteers; were there other community organisations and people able to offer counselling or support?

Following in the Footsteps of Others

When considering the kind of therapeutic response needed in Machynlleth I also drew on reports of projects established in traumatised communities across the world, including narrative therapists in Sri Lanka following the Indian Ocean tsunami of December 2004, and volunteer support workers in Atlanta following Hurricane Katrina in 2005.

Lara Pera was with a team in Sri Lanka. She offers the following advice, relating to her experience and the setting (Arulampalam, Perera, de Mel, White and Denborough 2005, 5-6):

1. To avoid medicalising people's responses.
2. To question the assumption that Sri Lankans as a group were "traumatised".
3. To return to normalcy.
4. To build on local resources and knowledge.
5. To be culturally sensitive.
6. To prioritise community participation and community empowerment.
7. To be inclusive of all members of the community.
8. To consider long-term sustainability.
9. To consider the ethics and real effects of research projects.
10. To share resources and information.

Although the effects of a tsunami are very different to the circumstances in which we found ourselves in Machynlleth, these principles in some ways felt very appropriate, and we used them to underpin the Listening Point project.

Setting up a "counselling" response implies that something is damaged and needs "mending" by experts. It was very important to us that we did not make assumptions that, as a group, the whole Machynlleth community had been traumatised, or that there was anything "abnormal" about how people were responding emotionally to their circumstances.

As a therapist who often works with trauma, I am very aware that, when asking people to speak about the events that have traumatised them, I should not do it in ways that re-traumatise. As Salter points out, when a person speaks about a traumatic memory they are liable to re-experience the same feelings and thoughts they had at the time of the traumatic event (Salter 1995).

For many of us in Machynlleth, April's disappearance transformed overnight the everyday experience of living in this beautiful location into one underlaid with fear and threat.

Lisa recalls:

> As well as the expert services conducting their search. I think everybody, as they went about their everyday lives was checking any areas they thought could possibly be hiding the remains of that precious little child.
>
> I know as a dog walker wandering through woods and forests, it was always uppermost in my mind: 'Would I have a phone signal if I came across the unthinkable?' I remember a house on one of our walks, which had been for sale for a while. I suggested to my husband that we check the outhouses.
>
> Even it seems a simple walk in the countryside became quite traumatic, because of what may be found.

The notion of "double listening" (White 2003) was also seen as important in hearing and responding to people's stories of what was happening in Machynlleth. The emotional distress we were experiencing could be re-framed from a "problem" to a tribute to "the person's refusal to be separated from the values, purposes, beliefs, hopes, dreams and commitments that are important to them" (ibid, 20). The fact that this missing child meant so much to so many people was perhaps a tribute to the values many of us held about life, childhood and living in Machynlleth.

West relates how, when working in Atlanta with the Red Cross, she was advised

> … not to think of the work as "doing therapy". She (the trainer) said we sometimes would be offering persons in the line a bottle of water or a snack, saying hello, and asking how the wait in line was going. Often, these practices of hospitality would establish a connection which would later enable a telling and a re-telling of people's experience (West 2005, 6).

She goes on to explain, that "when people feel comfortable and welcomed, they told stories. Not in a way of re-traumatising, but rather of creating a narrative account of survival in the midst of terror and chaos" (ibid, 7).

Hospitality was a very important aspect of our work at Listening Point – the offering of tea, cake, and biscuits. Out of this gentle, non-invasive approach emerged stories of people's lives that strengthened us all.

Chapter Two

Meeting the Press

"Invisible threads of hope are stronger
than all the chains that bind you."
—Friedrich Nietzsche

Sue's journal: 4th October 2012

My mobile bleeps: A message received.
"Could you give an interview to ITV Wales
to say how local people feel about this?"

As I listen, I switch on the TV.
April's parents' faces on the television.
Heart-breaking pleas for a speedy return.
"She's only little..." Echoes in my mind.

Frozen for a moment, I hesitate and hang up.
Afraid.
My attention is soon caught by the scene out of the window;
streams of people searching the hillside.

I witness from my window a small act of kindness;
the young woman gently touches the searcher's arm.
A mug of tea is proffered.

No words are exchanged;
just eye contact and compassion.

Community Update October 2012

2nd October 2012
"The Six O'clock News comes again live this evening from Machynlleth, where the police continue to search for little April Jones." (BBC1 News)

"The small town of Machynlleth (2,100 residents) has been inundated with national and international media and press, including 47 TV stations and all major newspapers." (BBC Radio 4)

3rd October 2012
17:30: "Police reveal the operation has been unprecedented in the UK in terms of scale and terrain. Neighbouring forces and specialist teams are helping with a focus on over 20 scenes around Machynlleth. The operation has led to 600 messages from the public to police, and the search involves 100 mountain rescue volunteers, 100 police specialist searchers, 20 dog handlers, as well as coastguards and two RNLI craft.

"It is confirmed that April has cerebral palsy and needs medication."

18:00: "Another vigil at St Peter's Church is held. The Right Reverend Andrew John, the Bishop of Bangor, said people 'all over the country are now praying for April's safe return'." (www.bbc.co.uk/news)

4th October 2012
10:00: "Volunteers gather for searches of 15 villages within a 10 to 15-mile radius of Machynlleth. Around 450 responded to a call from local search coordinators for people with 'good local knowledge' to search farmland and outbuildings."

11:00: "Police renew their appeal for information, no matter how small, from the public. They also want to know about suspect Mark Bridger's movements, as they are given more time to question him by Aberystwyth magistrates.

"There are around 500 volunteers in the area, who are thanked for their help but reminded that police must coordinate the search to ensure its integrity. Those with good local knowledge are asked to help search farmland and outbuildings.

"Prime Minister David Cameron said it was every family's nightmare. He urges anyone with information to speak to police, as does Welsh First Minister Carwyn Jones."

17:30: "Police say they received more than 2,500 calls in response to their latest appeal for information.

"They search a small farmhouse in the nearby village of Ceinws, where Mr Bridger was known to be living most recently.

"The town of Machynlleth is covered with pink ribbons in response to April's mother's appeal for people to wear her daughter's favourite colour." (www.bbc.co.uk/news)

Meeting the Media

One of the things that shocked me most on the first day following April's abduction was that the media were there so soon: so many satellite dishes; reporters all clamouring for information and the best angle for their news story. The residents of Machynlleth were, that first morning, trying to come to terms with the fact that a child had been abducted in the night from our town.

Anne Marie, an ethnographic film maker living in the town, who had been running the Ffilm Club project for young people from the Bryn-y-Gog estate, recalls:

My mind went back to the night.

The first searches;
as soon as we found out.

There was no police 'til the next day;
it didn't feel like they were there at all.
The police had got roadblocks out,
but when we were in the leisure centre...

There was one community policeman who turned up
about midnight;
but there were no police.

But there was a film crew from S4C.
By 11pm when we came back from the first search
there was a film crew.

There was a film crew. There so soon,
and I felt sick;
I felt physically sick.
I still feel sick.

I've thought quite a lot
about why I felt so sick,
(it was an S4C film crew,
although I didn't know who they belonged to at the time).
They weren't a big national broadcasting company;
there were two people with a small camera.

So very much how I might work, for example.
And they were "in there"
like lightning.
It felt like they were there before the police.

How did they know this was going on?
I guessed on the night it was S4C (and I was right)
But I wasn't really sure on the night.

It was...
Someone had talked to them.
And I just felt really sick.

And it was not just that they were there, a presence along with the police teams, but that they were broadcasting to an expectant audience across the world. Anne Marie again:

I was really torn because
the programme that S4C produced was out by the end of that week;
I think it was shown on the Thursday night.

I saw it, and I thought that some of it was really good.

They did a whole thing
where they invited an ex-police detective,
a Welsh guy,
to look around Bryn-y-Gog estate and assess its safety.
He pronounced that Bryn-y-Gog estate
was an extremely safe estate;
so no blame to attach to the parents;
which was brilliant.

But what was horrible about the programme,
apart from the speed with which it came out
(the cynicism in doing that made me feel sick);
but obviously, that's what TV does.

But the beginning and end of the programme
There was a little cameo shot of April,
and at the end

what they did
was (it was full size screen);
then they shrunk it into a black circle until it disappeared;
and then put her name on it;
as though she was dead.
And we did not know she was dead at the time of broadcast.

We did not know on that Thursday as we watched it,
because we did not find out until later that it was a murder investigation.

And really for me,
it was a massive thing,
because this was my working life, for so many years.

I never liked that side of it.
I never did it.

And that's why I didn't make a career in television;
because I couldn't.

I can't do that kind of programme making.
I can't justify it.

Most of us watch, listen to or read the news on TV, radio or in the newspapers. Many, like me, regard stories such as that of April's disappearance as factual accounts. Watching, I have always felt, gives me an opportunity to think about, and be concerned for, the communities affected – and in some cases enables me to help in some way (for example, by sending donations to a disaster appeal). However the experience of living in the glare of that media scrutiny was very different. As Lisa says:

> They appeared so quickly and with such fury, like a plague of locusts ready for a good juicy feed!
>
> It was inevitable that every TV news channel and newspaper wanted a reporter on the job; feeding it all to the eagerly awaiting public and boosting their ratings and sales.

When the overnight search for April turned into many days, the media settled in for a long stay. Local hotels and guesthouses filled up. Cafés and restaurants were full of strangers clutching microphones, television cameras, recorders and notebooks. This, combined with the horror of the story that was unfolding, left many of us feeling as if we had entered a "parallel universe" (North 2000).

One morning in the first week following April going missing I woke to the sound of three helicopters overhead, and one landed in the neighbouring playing fields. I counted 36 press vans, with their satellite dishes and crews, on my way into town (a quarter of a mile). The reporters were in the cafés and shops, interviewing. When you switch on the BBC News and see your own driveway as the backdrop to a live report, normality seems to slip into the surreal.

I was contacted via my counselling website by local and national newspapers and TV stations with requests to do numerous interviews, and ITV asked if I would be interested in them making a documentary about the Listening Point project. Most of these requests I politely refused as I felt that media coverage would compromise the confidentiality of the project. The interviews I did give were mainly to local papers where we advertised the opening hours and help- line telephone numbers.

Hope remembers:

> It started sort of slowly;
> the feelings that developed,
> they crept in bit by bit.
> The radio news was first to share
> the concept that could not be.

I stood alone at home and felt the harsh elements;
the places a little body could be hidden;
river, woodland,
my garden shed.

I feared that garden shed and what it might contain;
I couldn't look,
the dark and filthy terror stood waiting.

I remember helicopters searching overhead;
hours of vibrating desperation;
hope and energy.

The community rallied round;
local shops and services opened their doors and supported the searchers. Many local volunteers
but, increasingly,
strangers, paid professionals.

The town owned the tragedy as if it was their own;
they were fierce in their pursuit for a happy conclusion;
a safe home coming;
a settling back and a closing down to the quiet and the ordinary.

The hours and days went on;
more police and vans and strangeness.
The Wednesday market empty.
Camera crews,
bright lights,
a shock of intensity in those dark October days.

The tears come as I remember.
I am changed;
my world view is changed;
I have been made raw inside.
The church service on the Sunday, as I drove past,
a scene from a film set, camera, action.

It wasn't real, it couldn't be.

This was Machynlleth!
Not somewhere on TV where bad things happen.
I kept driving.
I wanted to escape.
I couldn't stand it anymore.

As a film-maker, Anne Marie was particularly sensitive to the behaviour of some of her professional peers:

And this is of course the reason I could not pick up a camera the whole time. If I tried, people locally were angry, and asked me if I worked for the media – as an accusation – so I couldn't possibly document anything as it was impossible to film and continue to be accepted as a member of the community.

I still can't pick up a camera to film events associated with April.
My doctoral supervisor is saying:
"Oh, they are knocking Mark Bridger's building down,
are you going to film it?"
NO.

I can't do that.
I cannot do that.
I haven't sat down and worked out exactly
why I can't film my film;
and actually of course at Ffilm club, the kids...
The stuff that has been filmed of local events;
the kids have all done it all.

And I wonder...
is that me just dumping the responsibility onto them?

I say to her:

No, I don't think so, because they are only filming things they want to film. There is something I am hearing, though, about your position as a film-maker and noticing the difference.

She replies:

There's definitely something in that.
I need to think about that.
But I just feel so sick thinking about that camera,
And then I had invested all my anger
around that whole event into
a particular reporter from Sky News
who interviewed people really badly in the town.
I lay awake all one night and then got up really early the next morning.
I went to work to get my camera and interview her.

I had made up my mind I was going to go and ask her
why she did her job,
and what she thought was valuable about all those sorts of questions.

I was incandescent with anger.
I got there
and she had been taken off the job.

Because she behaved so badly.
She was gone.
Which was really good.

But...
My avenue for revenge was gone too.

The more I think about the events in October and November 2012, the more convinced I am that the media had a huge effect both on how we as a community responded and on our physical and mental health. It even had an effect on those who were watching the footage at home.

I was surprised that the media coverage of events in Machynlleth prompted several calls to the helpline from people elsewhere in the UK who felt "traumatised" by the detailed coverage. I was interested to read an article about media coverage of terrorist acts in Israel. The authors state in their summary of the article:

> Shortly after a series of severe terrorist attacks had taken place in Israel, 534 people were asked to fill out a questionnaire that assessed their attitudes and reactions to the media's coverage of these acts as well as a questionnaire that examined their information-seeking style. The results

> suggested that, although a considerable proportion of media consumers preferred detailed coverage of terrorist acts, when the coverage included horrifying details, the readiness for receiving detailed information declined. In addition, the results indicated that exposure to such coverage was associated with the development of symptoms similar to those of Post-Traumatic Stress Disorder. (Keinan, Sadeh and Rosen 2003, 149).

It would seem that a careful balance has to be maintained for the benefit of both those living where the critical incident is occurring, and also the public at large.

There is a body of research into the effects of media coverage on communities experiencing traumatic events. Some research shows that the media reinforces certain aspects of a news story over and over again, and that this has been found to fuel anxiety (Vasterman, Yzermans and Dirkzwager 2005a). Vasterman and colleagues' review of media coverage of disasters and its effect on people's health concluded that:

> Media hypes are media-generated news waves reinforcing over and over again one specific frame while ignoring other perspectives. Such news waves can fuel fear and anxiety among people involved in one way or another in the aftermath of disasters. People tend to adopt the explanations offered by the media and integrate them into their story about their own health complaints. This tendency applies to people with endemic health problems as well as to patients with identifiable disease (Vasterman, Yzermans and Dirkzwager 2005b, 114).

A report on research into the effect of media broadcasting following the Boston Marathon bombings found that:

> Repeated bombing-related media exposure was associated with higher acute stress than was direct exposure. Media coverage following collective traumas can diffuse acute stress widely (Holman, Garfin and Silver 2014, 99).

In the UK, Jemphrey and Bennington considered that the press reporting of the Hillsborough disaster "added to the burden of grief of the bereaved through its hostile portrayal of Liverpool football supporters" (2000, 471). By contrast they note that the "coverage of the Dunblane shooting was markedly more compassionate" (ibid, 480). Also, this research highlighted complex issues relating to what they describe as the "political economy of news production" and "the regulatory mechanisms governing the press" (ibid, 480).

Mostly the media treated us with compassion, but I always felt uncomfortably aware that this could change at any time. Machynlleth was portrayed as a bereaved community in the grip of a terrible tragedy, but we too could very quickly have found ourselves pilloried if we failed to fit the stereotype.

Maria remembers:

The day after April went missing I got up very early, after a poor night, to walk my dog, and as I turned the corner into Bryn-y-Gog I saw the police tape and the TV vans and had a terrible jolt of shock as I really expected that she would have turned up safe and sound; it suddenly hit me that this was very serious.

During the first few days, like everyone else, I couldn't stop reading the papers and endlessly watching the news, hoping for something good, and as the months went on hoping for anything, desperate even for her body to be found, for some sort of resolution.

I hated the media for their intrusion, even though I was following it like everyone else, and I grew increasingly annoyed at the way Machynlleth was being turned into some sort of paragon of community life (I got to the stage where had I heard one more local person say "We are a small community with a big heart," I would have thrown something at the TV!).

I love this town and I do believe we are a good community but we are like any other small town – there are quarrels, resentments, difficulties and I always felt that, if something unpleasant came out, the media would knock us down as quickly as they had built us up.

I was also very uncomfortable at the way some of our community leaders, who were under a tremendous strain trying to hold us together and bring some comfort, were almost hounded into being minor celebrities; speaking for the town as a whole – a very dangerous position to be in, leaving them open to criticism as no one can ever represent the views of everyone.

Global press coverage also generates a lot of interest from around the world, which can be experienced as both positive and negative. In Mick North's personal account of his experience of the Dunblane school shootings, he comments:

> The massacre sent waves of shock and horror around the world. Waves of sympathy and love rolled back. Those of us who'd lost loved ones would not grieve alone, but neither would we be able to (North 2000, location1720).

He continues:

> The victims were no longer our children: they were seen now as angels, God's children and they'd become Dunblane's children, more a part of the community than they had been when alive (location 1726).

This resonates with what happened in Machynlleth following April's murder. The media coverage prompted messages of sympathy to the family, police and to the Listening Point project from all over the world. Within days Machynlleth became "that town where the little girl went missing" and, indeed, for many of us in the community April became "our child". The offers of help flooded in. As Jeremy Josephs points out in relation to the murder of 16 people in Hungerford in August 1987: "In fact there were so many offers of help that the vicarage soon had someone working in every room" (Josephs 1993: 1531)

It was good to receive so much support from around the world, but sometimes it felt quite a burden; we certainly could not, as North points out from Dunblane, "grieve alone".

I was all too aware that some of those watching the reports on their televisions were in some ways being "traumatised" by what they saw, as Holman and colleagues (Holman, Garfin and Silver 2014) describe in their study of the media's role following the Boston Marathon bombings. I received emails and calls to the helpline from across the UK, and beyond, from people who had personal experience of losing a child or had themselves been abused as a child, or who had lived with violent partners.

Some of the reporters who were with us day after day also became visibly upset and anxious about the situation.

Anne Marie recalls:

I found a centre called DART[1] (I think?)
who look after traumatised journalists.
It was from the minutes of a conference following the Soham murders.

The journalists who were there said it was so traumatic because
the people wanted you there
to help publicise the case and hopefully find the girls.
And then,
two weeks later when they found their bodies,
they just wanted you gone.
You were no longer of any use,
just an intrusion and a reminder.

They said that it just "makes you feel so useless".
The journalists were really traumatised by that.
I really understood that.

Because the massed media had such a negative effect on our ability for normalcy, a key criteria for our drop-in was that it should be, in the words of one volunteer, "a press-free oasis".

Initially, in our first location in the St Peter's Church office, this was not the case. We were on the main high street and on one occasion a journalist knocked at the door. Although he was very polite and respectful, it felt like a physical intrusion. I remember trying to position my body in the doorway so that I blocked his view of the room. We were all left feeling vulnerable and rather exposed.

Lisa remembers:

At the Listening Point we all became a little edgy, suspicious of all who might be a reporter walking through the door. One person even commented they felt akin to being violated in some way.

Through the window we could see white press vans passing by and large microphones and interviewing equipment being set up on

---

[1] Dart Center for Journalism and Trauma. A resource for journalists who cover violence http://dartcenter.org/overview

the street, hoping to catch some poor innocent passer-by to gather a few snippets of information regarding the horrific set of circumstances unfolding in this little Welsh town.

When we moved to a new premises on the Bryn-y-Gog estate we were also located within the hub of press activity. We were however protected here by a police embargo. The police had negotiated with the media, to give regular updates and interviews and, in return, the press were not permitted to film April's family, or our building, or interview or film any people coming or going from this building. This was largely respected. It often felt like we were an island surrounded by media activity; but they became such a regular feature that we were on the whole able to ignore them.

However, as Lisa also recalls, the media presence persisted and, indeed, returned long after the police activity had ended.

As time passed, their presence sadly became as familiar as the police vans with tracker dogs moving around the area, together with divers and helicopters.

After the trial and conviction of mark bridger (he does not deserve his name with capitals), when the teams had stood down and finally left town; the press still kept returning to cover an anniversary or birthday of little April.

On one such occasion, Hope was coming to meet me at the drop-in and had to run the gauntlet of the press who were back in force, following an absence of some weeks. Two TV vans followed her as she drove up to the building and she came in, stressed and distressed.

She tells me:

I want to say to them:

"Do you know how this feels?"

"Do you know how this feels?"

I feel...
So angry.

Angry... not just with them.

I say:

With me also I guess?
Do you want to go out and shout at them,
at me,
for suggesting we meet here?

Hope replies:

It feels really uncomfortable;
It really hurts.
I just feel
so tired
and battered with it all.

I just feel "not again".
My sense of equilibrium is upset.

I am shocking myself;
there is a feeling of... "out of control"!
I am shocking myself.

I am angry with them, with you.
There is ambivalence;
sometimes
there is this feeling of
I really don't want to be here.

I just want to go away.
Sorry Sue.

Yet this project, being here at the drop-in,
has been amazing.
I love being part of it.

I just love it.
Being part, and with people I feel I have come to really know.
I want to stay with these feelings;
not brush them away.
They are important to feel.

I tell her:

Stay with the feelings,
It is ok to have these feelings.
Acknowledging and accepting them is ok;
working through them feels really important.

We talk for some time. At the end Hope says:

I feel very different now.
The anger has gone.
I can look at them (points to the press vans) outside
and it is ok.
It is about moving on.

As time passes, there is a very healthy desire to move forward and not to be trapped by the media's interpretation of "the tragedy of Machynlleth" (Daily Mail, 23 October 2013). And, indeed, I hope my account will be interpreted as a story of hope rather than one of tragedy.

But at the time I tell Hope:

I am left however with a feeling of being caged in – this is not ok. It will never be ok to have the press in the car park.

How can we move on, hemmed in by the press and their expectations of us?

Grief, and grieving for a child, is a complex and very unique experience however (Videka-Sherman 1982). What helps one person who is grieving will not necessarily help another. There were people within the community who had a very different outlook towards the media and had regular contact, giving interviews and updates; keeping the search for April in public awareness. It was important, I felt, that whatever our own feelings, we were able to respect both of these positions.

The Social Media

Smith (2010) researched the role of the social media (in this case, Twitter) following the 2010 earthquake in Haiti. He points out:

> Social media and communication technology have shifted the power of communication from public relations practitioners to social media users who may not have a recognized role or defined interest in an organization. What results is a social model of public relations in which traditional public relations responsibilities are distributed to social media users, and which depends on interactivity, legitimacy, and a user's social stake (Smith 2010, 488).

Whereas it used to be the prerogative of the international media and governments to control what news we as consumers received, news travels speedily now via the social media networks. This can have advantages, as in the early days following April's disappearance when volunteers were drafted within hours to join the search. It also enabled friends of April's family to offer support. This is demonstrated by Dabner (2012) in a case study showing how social media supported a university population following the 2010 earthquake on South Island, New Zealand:

> The findings propose that social media can effectively support information sharing, communication and collaboration in higher education contexts, in particular in times of crisis (Dabner 2012, 69).

Social media coverage can, however, be unhelpful in several ways. In Machynlleth most of the volunteers from outside the area came out of love and solidarity, but I think their numbers added an extra burden to the police teams and made more difficult their attempts to preserve evidence and integrity for ongoing investigations.

Myth can also be published, as well as fact. For example, the "find April Jones" Facebook page recorded messages of hope and help from across the world. But in December 2012, long after the search had become a murder investigation, it still had an open profile and was being messaged by many people in an outpouring of support and hope for April's safe return. I am sure the page provided solace for many but, with a man arrested for April's murder, it added to the confusion that many in the community felt. The site has now become a "closed group" but it still has over 2,000 members.

Photos taken on mobiles and tablets were sent streaking across the world, sometimes accurately reflecting the situation, but at other times making a difficult situation worse.

People living locally were bombarded with “friend” requests from those wanting an “inside view” of the situation, including undercover reporters.

Considerations and conclusions

In any traumatic community event, whether it is a child going missing or some other kind of disaster or tragedy affecting a community, it would seem to be important to take into consideration the role of the media. If you are setting up a project like Listening Point, it is important to ensure you have someone (either the press officer of a hosting charity or police press officers) who will negotiate with the media on your behalf. In Machynlleth we were very fortunate in that we had the support of the police teams press officer and the Church in Wales press officer. It is worth considering how you are going to ensure media co-operation.

The following points may be helpful.

- The media may be useful in helping to promote your service, but don’t forget that they will have their own agenda, which may not always match your own. Some will use underhand tactics to get what they want. For example, a member of our team was asked casually by a visitor “Do you know where April lived? I want to drop off a letter of support?” They were in fact tabloid journalists.

- Community members may be traumatised by the media presence, but journalists may themselves be traumatised by the event they are covering.

- People from across the UK and world may also be affected by the unfolding story and may contact your support service for help.

- Social media is good for providing information quickly to large numbers of people and for broadcasting calls for volunteers, but you cannot control what people do with the information they read, and its accuracy.

- The viral spread of knowledge worldwide can brings benefits but also challenges when it becomes overwhelming. The response to your calls for help may be greater than you need.

- Where there is an ongoing police investigation, it is very important that any proposed support service is discussed with community leaders and police teams. As well as the benefits of a shared vision of what a potential service might look like and how people can be referred, it will also enable you to devise a more effective media management strategy. Without the support of the police and other community leaders we would have struggled, especially in our relationships with the media.

CHAPTER THREE

STARTING POINT FOR A NEW PROJECT

Sue's journal: 26 October 2012

I feel confused. Around me the search efforts for April have been doubled. Mountain rescue teams scour the surrounding hillside; waves of them can be seen in the unrelenting leafless landscape; picking over each blade of grass and tree root. Divers continue to search the turbulent river. There is a sense of urgency; desperation even. Forensic teams can still be seen at Mark Bridger's house. Press vans and news reporters continue to give ongoing updates to a waiting world.

Yet, within all of this activity a man, a local man who is known personally by many, and by sight by many more, has been arrested for murder. In response to the charge he has said, "I think I probably killed her." Nothing makes sense – some people are convinced April is still alive and waiting to be found. Social media streams messages by the hundred saying "Do not give up hope," "Your beautiful little girl will be found." Police statements seem enigmatic: "Yes, the searching will go on."

The people living here seem to be withdrawing, rushing into shops and buying necessities. "I feel so guilty at even buying normal things" one woman tells me. Smiling seems somehow impossibly disloyal to April's family. I finally make an appointment to meet the Police Welfare Officer. I wonder if there is anything I can do to help; surely they must have some plans afoot for supporting people.

My hands shake as I walk through the temporary office doors of the temporary police command centre; I want to turn and walk away. I am, however, ushered up to a room that I have used frequently for counselling. The man, the police welfare officer greeting me, looks exhausted; I agree to a cup of tea as he looks as if he needs one.

He has been working 12-hour days (with a couple of hours travelling time) for the last four weeks. He confirms that he is supporting both the task forces and the volunteers. He also tells me what provisions have been put in place for the local schools, and that a counsellor contracted to offer sessions in Newtown has not been used. "What is needed,' he says, "is for somewhere that local people can meet together and talk." His observation tallies with my own thoughts, in that he considers morale higher while the local volunteers were "doing something and meeting together".

Community Update November 2012

1 November 2012
"More than £35,000 has been raised for April's Fund by the local community.

"Hundreds of people turned out to see a town clock lit up in pink to mark the third week of April's disappearance.

"Mr and Mrs Jones also said, 'We have taken great strength from the procession through the town to the church and the lighting up of the town clock in pink, April's favourite colour.'

"A community member says, 'I think as a whole community we have hope and we have to carry on having hope because you just can't give up.'"
(www.bbc.co.uk/news

As October 2012 drew to a close, I observed a visible and tangible closing down of the vibrant creative community in which I lived. People hurried across the town, heads down, doing only what was absolutely necessary. Hope remembers:

My senses felt heightened in the beginning – the mood of the community and town, the helicopters flying overhead, endlessly searching, looking, hoping. The call to search, the camaraderie, the love and distress openly shown, the joining of forces for a common good. I felt it all and lived through those first few days praying she would be found alive, but scared to look in my own shed and storage bunker, just in case it was the one that had been chosen to hide the precious little April, the tiny little schoolgirl.

The cameras came, and Sky News came; I saw it on the television: our little town, the streets I walk, my favourite shops, the estate agent I worked in only a few months ago. Exposed for the entire world to see, to stare at, to make comments on. I felt they knew nothing about us. I felt angry, exhausted with the exposure, not wanting to go into the town. I took to staying in more and lighting a candle, as if that would keep the hope alive. I look back and feel bitter at what the truth of it was. Mark Bridger, the cruel and heartless monster, had extinguished this precious life. I hated him; I hate him still; I think I can admit to myself that a part of me probably always will. I am not proud of this, as I know I need to forgive him in some way, but I am human and this I feel I must allow myself. The anger rages in me still; it is easily felt and glimpsed. It is still as if a core of fire within me sears and seethes in quite a menacing way;, it is not in my control, but I hope as time passes it will grow smaller.

Then, after a time, a level of protection came over my whole being; my body, my emotions and senses. I felt myself "shut down"; the horrible truth was coming to the surface and all the levels of horrendous deeds done. The experience had become alive for me – a creature dark and menacing that crept around the townsfolk and tormented and threatened their very souls. Some may call it evil, others wanted to kill; I felt paralysed and shocked; I knew my life would never be the same.

I felt quite alone, my loved ones not really wanting to talk too much about the unfolding experience, the disgusting details. I, within my counselling practice, reached out to those needing help and healing, space and support. I know this role; it is safe for me, but what about my own darkness; how could I connect with that and feel part of the whole community experience? Then it happened; the very embodiment of what I needed presented itself to me; I found myself involved in the Listening Point drop-in. I didn't realise just how much being part of this wonderful group of volunteers would truly mean.

Lisa moved to Machynlleth in the spring of 2012. She remembers:

April 2012; that is when we moved to Wales, Machynlleth being some 12 miles from our tiny hamlet of Cwm Cewydd. Oh, how soon we were all to become so sadly familiar with the name "April".

Six months on and we were busy settling into our new home and exploring the area, as it was all pretty unfamiliar to us. The chilling evening of 1st October will be emblazoned in everybody's memory forever.

Machynlleth was on the radar, hitting the news in such a tragic and terrible way. The disappearance of a little five-year-old girl called April Jones, from the Bryn-y-Gog estate. A simple treat of being allowed to play out on her bike with friends a little later after having a glowing report at parents evening, turned into the unthinkable set of circumstances. The fear, in the back of every parent's mind, suddenly was becoming reality for the family of little April.

The searching began, combing vast areas of hazardous and dangerous terrain. The town of Machynlleth was united in a state of shock, disbelief and utter despair that such a thing could happen, let alone here. Community spirit was quite amazing and overwhelming, with people coming from all over Wales and England to help in whatever capacity they could. Messages of support poured in from all over the globe. Pink ribbons began to appear attached to any available object – April's favourite colour. An all too familiar sight was that of divers searching the rivers, trackers with dogs and the noise of the helicopters overhead.

My initial assessment of the need at the time of April's abduction was that it was too soon to provide a "counselling service" and that, although it would be good to have counselling referral resource available, the most immediate need was for a safe place where people could meet and talk, and a helpline for those unable to get to the centre, or who wanted privacy to talk through their feelings about the ongoing events. The helpline would also signpost people to the counselling service, police, GP or drop-in, as appropriate.

Developing a plan

Consultation also with colleagues and my clinical supervisor confirmed that we didn't necessarily need just trained counsellors to work with individuals, but a more community-based listening and support service. I then began to think about what kind of therapeutic model would be most helpful.

In my own work I use an integrative therapeutic model. My initial training was in person-centred counselling and I could see that Carl Rogers' core conditions (which he saw as necessary for therapeutic work) of empathy, unconditional positive regard and acceptance (Rogers 1961) would be needed if we were to "stand alongside" others. I could also see benefit in using the narrative therapy approaches in which I had recently become very interested. These are described by Michael White as "maps of practice" (White 2007a) that help the therapist orientate herself within ways of working that see reality as socially constructed through our relationships and the stories we tell of those relationships. The goal of narrative therapy is remarkable simple: to enable people to develop thicker richer stories to describe their life experiences (White and Epston 1990).

Machynlleth in November 2012 seemed to be trapped within a "tragedy" narrative; the on-going shocking events and press coverage meant that even those not directly involved felt trapped. There seemed no other story that could, or should, exist, and this was leading to feelings more normally associated with trauma; for example, anxiety, panic, flashbacks and nightmares. One resident reported that her daughter had asked her to take a picture of her in her party dress "in case I go missing and you need to find me". An elderly lady reported dreaming every night of being out searching on the wooded hillside. Others reported a sense of "dread and foreboding" and unexplained panic accompanied by physiological symptoms such as sweating nausea and pain.

Using this kind of narrative therapy approach would, I hoped, not seek to "cure individuals" of post-traumatic symptoms but, rather, would support and enable the community to re-engage with each other and create other stories to tell about their lives here in Machynlleth. It would be helpful, I felt, to have some trained counsellors available to undertake one-to-one sessions with individuals, but we would also need volunteers who would be willing just to listen and to learn new ways of being with people.

Liaising with Others

Towards the end of October 2012 I approached CAMAD (Community Action Machynlleth and District) and the local churches. I was looking for volunteers to help with the project, especially the drop-in. I was also interested in what other community leaders and individuals thought about was needed at this time, and if they knew of people who would be "good listeners" and might be interested in being involved.

At the same time I was thinking about how to fund such a project and what kind of governance might be needed. I put out feelers to a counselling charity, the Churches Counselling Service in Wales, for which I was then working as a volunteer, to see if they would host the project and provide us with both governance and charitable status. I compiled a business plan, with expected costs, including premises, utilities and expenses for volunteers, and to my relief the trustees were very supportive.

Funding for the project was not a problem: Machynlleth was in the public eye and people and organisations wanted to "do something" to help us. Our initial start-up funding came in swiftly from the Welsh Presbyterian Church, The Church in Wales (both of whom were major stakeholders and funders of the Churches Counselling Service in Wales) and the Iona Community (of which I am a member).

As previously noted, the local Church in Wales (St Peter's) offered the use of their parish office for the drop-in centre (the office was on the High Street, in a building that had previously been used as a shop).

CAMAD helped to advertise for volunteers, and I also advertised via community social media (Machynlleth Swap-Shop). I booked a venue for a meeting early in November 2012.

The day of the meeting dawned and, to my amazement, the room was full. Twenty-six people turned up, and all of them listened intently to what I was suggesting. I was very anxious but soon overcame my nerves and set out my thoughts on what might be needed. Gradually they started to tell me their reasons for wanting to be involved. I remember feeling a jumble of emotions: terror at the enormity of the task, sad that this was real, but also relieved that I was no longer alone in this.

June writes:

My experience of it began by responding to a simple request from you to be involved in a charity outreach to people in need of talking to someone with a caring ear. I would be up for that, to extend my own desire to be a more sympathetic and responsive person. There was much anguish resonating in the town resulting from a recent shocking tragedy.

Another couple of experienced counsellors working in the area also offered support and advice on how the drop-in, helpline and counselling service should be managed and supervised. Cruse Powys (who had been supporting the primary school in Machynlleth) also agreed to provide some initial listening skills training for the volunteers.

The training was in two parts: I offered basic listening skills training and Cruse ran workshops on further listening skills and bereavement support. The training sessions continued throughout the life of the project, with experienced practitioners giving their time to run free workshops on various aspects of trauma, bereavement and counselling.

Practical issues

Volunteers brought in tablecloths, soft furnishings, books, jigsaws. Gradually we were able to transform an empty hall into a welcoming, bright café-style space, with a vibrant children's corner, a "bring and share" book area and a small break-out room for anyone needing private space.

The hosting charity helped with translating posters and flyers about the forthcoming service into both English and Welsh and other volunteers were drafted in to deliver them door to door in the town and surrounding villages. This proved to be very time consuming, but also fruitful. My husband John, who volunteered for this job, found himself listening to many stories of how recent events had affected individuals. It was also a much more physically challenging task than we had anticipated – even in a small town such as Machynlleth there are many steps, hills and difficult letterboxes!

Concurrently I worked with the hosting charity to ensure that we had appropriate safeguarding policies and procedures and that the hosting charity's existing public and professional liability insurance would cover our activities. It was challenging to marry the dynamic needs of this new project with the more traditional approach of the host service, but the trustees put their trust in my skills as a manager.

We also decided to recruit two volunteer counsellors (in training) so that we could offer counselling to people who needed a series of counselling sessions, rather than the one-off sessions we could offer during drop-in sessions. To this end I approached the local counselling training provider and soon had applications from several final year students looking for placements. It was hoped that this counselling service would operate alongside, and take referrals from, the helpline and drop-in. We felt it was important however that the volunteer counsellors should receive independent clinical supervision, so I also set about recruiting an experienced counselling supervisor to take on this role. Keeping the services separate, yet working in tangent, should ensure the best possible service for clients, and enable people to access both the counselling service and the drop-in without the complications of dual roles.

Attention was also given to how we were going to staff and operate the help-line, the hours it may need to be available, and how we would staff it. So, we ordered the installation of a new land line (initially at my home) and also a mobile phone (to which we could divert calls).

I met with the police, including the police family liaison officers supporting April's family, to discuss our plans, as we wanted them to know what we were doing. The police were very supportive of our initiative, as were April's parents. We also obtained the support of local counsellors, businesses and organisations, who gave generously in various ways: by donating goods, services and/or putting up posters. Meanwhile, I started to receive requests from newspapers and TV companies for interviews. Where I was able to publicise the project and had editorial control over what was published, I agreed to write articles, as this gave us some free advertising. Other requests for interviews I declined.

The beginnings of richer, thicker descriptions

Meeting with the volunteers I was struck by their amazing skills and the knowledge they already held about the local community and how to cope with traumatic situations.

Already they were, in the words of Denborough and colleagues, "taking whatever action is possible, in their own ways, based on particular skills and knowledges, to try to address the effects of the problem(s) on their lives and the lives of those they love and care about" (Denborough et al. 2006, 20) – as were many others within the community.

As we started to meet it became clear that we were more able to stand alongside April's family and support each other when we came together in this way. When we were alone, many of us reported withdrawing and feeling "helpless and hopeless". So often when a crisis happens "the professionals" take over and manage the crisis. It felt very important that I was not seen as "the professional who would fix it" – a task I would have felt incapable of fulfilling, and which would have ignored the skills and knowledge of those around me. In retrospect I recognise that, despite all my efforts, I was to an extent always "the professional", but I hoped that by seeking to "enable others" rather than "fix the problem", I avoided creating a hierarchy of knowledge (based on academic learning), and respected the skills and local knowledge of those around me.

Gradually, over time, as we learned to make use of the de-briefing sessions, we shared stories about our lives and experiences. We had all, I realised, survived much, and this knowledge, and the ways in which we had survived in previous situations, strengthened both our bonds with each other and our ability to empathise and stand alongside the people who came for support. For many of the volunteers the de-briefing sessions felt very alien – a "baring of the soul when we are used to being private" as June comments. She goes on to write:

> Debriefing sessions proved traumatic in themselves for people not yet confident to "bare their chests". However, these particular sessions did nurture a bonding between fellow volunteers and very gradually they revealed little chinks, tender spots and anxieties lying deep within the bonding members.

It seemed important to keep the principles of narrative therapy in mind:

- **Re-membering conversations** that are shaped by "the conception that identity is founded on an 'association of life' rather than on a core self" (White 2007a, 129).

If our sense of identity is formed through our relationship with others then it should be possible to revise and review our relationships with others – both people in the here and now and also past relationships and significant others – even those we have never met (for example, literary figures or fictional characters), and bring to the fore the relationships that sustain us and let go of our attachment to the relationships that are harmful.

For example, I asked Sarah (a counselling client) to tell me more about her life. She spoke a lot about her late husband who had been "very controlling" and her father, whom she experienced as "dominant and bullying". In passing she also mentioned visiting an elderly neighbour who used to listen to her and let her walk his dog: "He encouraged me that anything was possible." I asked her to tell me more and discovered that this elderly man had been a really important figure in her young life, and had enabled her to carry on having confidence in herself. She had forgotten all about him, but as she told stories about their relationship she was able to add him to the list of people who had "been influential" in her life, and this gave her what she described as "stronger roots to be the person I want to be" (Dale 2011).

- **Re-authoring conversations** that invite people to continue to develop and tell stories about their lives, but also help people to include some of the more neglected but potentially significant events and experiences that are "out of phase" with their dominant storyline. These events and experiences can be considered "unique outcomes" or "exceptions" that provide a starting point for re-authoring conversations (White 2007b, 61).

For example, Joy, who consulted me some years ago, had lived her life with a diagnosis of mental illness. She still lived with her parents, but occasionally had to be admitted to psychiatric hospital. In later years this mental illness had been named as schizophrenia. She had been told that "Pip", whose company she had experienced for many years, was "negative", and doctors had spent much time trying to "eradicate him from my memory". However, within a therapeutic setting Joy started to talk about ways that Pip, although rather startling, had made her life possible and enabled her to engage with the world. She also started to notice that there were times when she did not need Pip to stand alongside her, and these were times when others did not judge or make fun of her. She started also to talk about her love of singing and how she found it very easy to pick up melodies from the radio. To start with these threads of alternative story were thin, but as she explored and built on them she began to gain confidence in her ability. She emailed me some time after we ceased to meet to tell me that she was now living independently and enjoying many community activities, including singing in a choir (Dale 2013).

- **Absent but implicit** is an expression used by Michael White to differentiate between what we speak about and give meaning to in our life experience and the stories we leave in the background and do not talk about (Carey, Walther and Russell 2009).

For example, Machynlleth is rich in heritage and creativity. Owain Glyndwr formed the first Welsh Parliament here. It is home to the Centre for Alternative Technology, pioneers since the early 1970s of eco solutions to life's challenges. There is a vibrant musical community, with several singing groups and choirs and the tabernacle music festival. It is the home to MOMA Wales, which hosts exhibitions of modern art and the UK Comedy Festival, not to mention the regular El Suano Latin American and Welsh Festival of Arts.

However, the only story told about Machynlleth in late 2012/2013 was the murder of April Jones.

White, while acknowledging the importance of witnessing and accepting the story being told, saw opportunity in finding out about the "absent but implicit", as these stories may give clues to how the current crisis can be overcome, or point to what the person values and why the perceived problem seems so insurmountable.

It was interesting that in Machynlleth, as people talked to me about how they felt about April's murder, a multitude of different feelings emerged, ranging from anger that "We moved here because it was a safe place to bring up our children, and now it is not" to "I was sexually abused as a child and the memories have come flooding back" or "I cannot bear to think what would happen if my own child were taken". It seemed important to enable people to connect again with those stories, which were attuned with their values, and to create links between their thoughts, feelings and histories.

Our first steps in sharing our own stories and re-membering' and re-authoring' our own experiences (White 2007a) meant that a previously absent but implicit story of "hope" started to emerge. It was a story of resilience and resistance to the evil encountered when Mark Bridger abducted and murdered a small child.

We volunteers met together even when we did not have any visitors and by doing so offered a visible alternative to the predominating narrative of "tragedy" playing out around us. We did not want to diminish the impact of what happened, or ignore the pain, but we did want to avoid becoming trapped and without connection to other life events.

Some in the community (who did not visit regularly) commented that they were "so glad you are there – I know you are there if I need you and that is really good". Others came occasionally, bringing gifts of cakes and books or just dropped in to see if we needed anything; others became our regulars.

Hope writes of the drop-in centre:

I feel it is a place I can belong but in my own particular way. A place I can get to know others in a gentle, bit by bit, risking and withdrawing kind of way. This level is very sincere for me and fills a space inside unfilled before. I feel a shared connection of joy and pain, of anger and confusion. The group itself is strong and robust and yet sensitive and gentle to its own and others' needs. I speak as if it lives as if it is a creature born from a tragedy, and I think for me that's what it is. Perhaps a creature of a higher power; is this what can be created in the name of good, love and truth? I think for me it is and I am thankful for it.

Considerations and conclusions

With the benefit of hindsight, there are several things that we might have done differently.

- Although it was very convenient and expedient to tie in the project into an existing charity that already used volunteer counsellors to provide a service, the dynamic needs of the project did not always tie in with the host organisation's models of operation, and this at times caused conflict. It was less time consuming than setting up a new charity however which was important given the crisis situation we were faced with.

- St Peter's Church office was situated on the main high street and was perceived by many as "church", and that deterred some potential visitors. It was also very difficult to see inside the office before entering. When we moved to our second location one visitor remarked: "Here I can see what is going on inside before I come in. At the other place it took a bit more courage to burst through the door."

- Delivering leaflets by hand had the advantage of being cheaper than the post office providing the service, and it provided an opportunity to talk with people and listen to their concerns, but it was very time consuming. The people delivering leaflets might benefit from some listening skills training.

CHAPTER FOUR

THE BEGINNING OF A RESEARCH PROJECT

Sue's journal: 27th November 2014
We met today, the five of us. Gathered in an upper room, around the teapot as usual. I outline my thoughts so far on the book and the contact I have had with various publishers. I want to get it right: to ensure we tell the story of the project without damaging ourselves or others.

We share news and then memories bubble up: the fun day with hotdogs cooking in the tea urn – "We could have given everyone food-poisoning;" "What would health and safety say?" "We were always laughing… Do you remember how people were surprised by that?" We laugh together. It was laughter that so often filled the centre with a "lightness" so different from outside the door. I look around me and cannot imagine a life where I will not be inspired by these wonderful women. Maria, who is not here today, but is always with us in our hearts, her compassionate listening skills hovering in the room. Hope, who lives up to her name, has come straight from work; she wants to write to somehow process what we have achieved together. Lisa, as always, is enthusiastic, and we drink in her energy and fire. Anne Marie looks tired – too much work that isn't paid, and Ceri, whose stillness and words we drink in, remembers "the young boys who turned into men overnight". She reminds us of the day we offered a creative session and she, myself and two young boys sat round a table painting large stones. The aim was to add these to the developing April's Garden. I was painting pictures of the volunteers – not well, but with love. Ceri explains, "The young boys (who are usually so active) sat so still, concentrating so hard, trying their very best to 'do something'." There was something about their earnestness. One boy said, "April was my friend. I saw her that evening." He painted her pink bicycle onto the stone. I feel tears prickle in my eyes at the memory, just as they did then. I look at my friends round the table. "Perhaps another time we will record our conversations?" I ask. Lisa speaks of how painting stones suddenly went viral – two young women from the estate asked if they could have a table over the holiday so that the children could keep painting. She brought in crates of flat Welsh slate stones that she had excavated from a stream, and which were duly painted and distributed around both April's Garden and the hugging tree (a tree which had been adorned with pink knitting from the local community in tribute to April).

Community update November 2012

10th November 2012
"Still the search for April goes on.

"Police and mountain rescue teams still scour the hillside whilst forensic teams have been undertaking searches of farm buildings, septic tanks and garden ponds." (Cambrian News)

Looking back at the events since 2012 and our response to them, I was certain that we needed somehow to capture something of both the experience of living through such a difficult time in Machynlleth's history and of setting up the Listening Point project. With respect to the latter, my hope was that if we could somehow evaluate, or quantify, what was helpful about the project, and indeed what might have been better, then we could leave some kind of legacy for other communities where tragedy strikes. With respect to the former, if we were able to articulate in a meaningful way something of our "lived experience" of this time, then this could inform other communities and the teams set up to support them when a crisis or tragedy strikes.

Two research questions came to my mind:

- what helps communities to cope with a traumatic event, and
- what helped us here in Machynlleth to cope?

To try to find an answer to the former I have read much literature relating to major events such as the 9/11 attack on the World Trade Center in New York; to particular communities affected by genocide, such as the Jews in World War II; and to countries such as Rwanda and the Democratic Republic of Congo. This literature underpins much of what is discussed in later chapters of this book.

With respect to what happened here in Machynlleth, I have wondered also whether the effects of trauma on a small community are different to those on a large city or country. I looked therefore at literature emanating from the UK, and research relating to rural communities.

When considering how to research the Listening Point project, I was aware that different kinds of research would give a different insight. For example, a large, quantitative study such as a randomised controlled trial to research the effectiveness of a new drug, medication or intervention may give a very good overview of a group of people's responses to treatment and give a "wide-angled view" of the overall situation. If, however, I wanted to investigate the particular moments of lived experience from people's individual perspectives, then a more microscopic view would be needed and qualitative research would be more effective. I, and the other volunteers, felt that we provided a professional service and adapted very swiftly to changing circumstances, but we did not really have time to process our own emotional responses to what had happened. To remain congruent with the therapeutic nature of the project, it seemed imperative that we use this research opportunity to also explore and try to "make sense" of what had happened and where we were now.

In view of the research questions and deliberations outlined above, it felt important to look at the quantitative data that we collected on attendance at the drop-in and use of the helpline. But I wanted also to understand more about the particular moments of lived experience of those using and working in the project, so a qualitative research methodology seemed a good choice.

I chose to use a collaborative narrative methodology. I wanted it to be congruent with the narrative approaches to therapy that we used in the project and to make the process of the research as transparent and collaborative as possible. I hoped that, although the research process was not overtly setting a therapeutic agenda, it might prove therapeutic to those involved, as had happened with past narrative projects in which I had been involved (Dale 2013, 2010,; 2011), and in other such research projects (Etherington 2001).

Narrative approaches to research

There are many different approaches to the use of narrative within research (Clandinin and Connelly 2000). Many social science researchers now use narrative research to great effect (Etherington 2000, 2007; Speedy 2005; Speedy and Wyatt 2014b).

Narrative research and the term "narrative inquiry" can have a variety of meanings, depending on the researcher's world view. At one end of the spectrum is the structuralist approach, where the researcher analyses the narratives they have collected in order to find correlations and perhaps the "truth" about particular circumstances or interventions. At the other end are researchers like me, who see the narrative as the research – we have a socially constructed understanding of reality. I see the emerging narratives created with the collaborators and the writing of them (Richardson 2000a, 2000b, 1990, 2003, 1992) as both the research process and the research outcome.

Clough, however, makes a very interesting observation that

> … narrative is useful only to the extent that it opens up (to its audiences) a deeper view of life in familiar contexts: it can make the familiar strange, and the strange familiar (Clough 2002, 8).

I hope that through the co-construction of the narratives of our experience of living and working in Machynlleth we will indeed make the "strange" world we found ourselves in familiar to others and enable us, to whom it became familiar, to look at these experiences in a different way.

Before turning to the specifics of our research process and the researchers' story, I should say a little more about my view of social constructionism and how this affects research.

Socially constructed identity and narrative research

Gallant points out that the accounts we tell of events are (un)performable because the events themselves have already been performed "as a constitutive part of my own life" (Gallant 2014, 70). The stories we tell of Machynlleth will only be our stories of the events that happened between 2012 and 2014. We can only give the reader our interpretation recalled at a distance from the events themselves.

Sarbin, whom Gallant cites, proposes:

> The built and natural environments provide a multiplicity of stages upon which people engage each other in dramatic interactions. Such

> engagements are the raw materials for building life-narratives from which identities are formed (Sarbin 2005, 205).

If we consider therefore that lives are socially constructed and that we construct our identity through the relationships we have with others and the stories that we tell of those relationships, then surely it would follow that constructing new community narratives about events, such as the community's responses to the murder of April Jones, would not necessarily be just a dispassionate "reporting" of those events but would lead us to a different understandings. The contributors and author, who have all lived through this together and experienced the events from our oqn perspective, may now find ourselves engaged in an altogether different narrative.

The narrative research reported here aims to "show" a dynamic process of research in action, through conversation and writing, rather than a "telling" of a research process that has happened. I have, as Clough states, tried

> … to blur distinctions not only between form and content, but also between researcher and researched, between data and imagination; to insist, that is, that language itself, by itself, does the work of inquiry, without recourse to the meta-languages of methodology (Clough 2002, 3).

Our stories contained within this narrative follow the events as they unfolded in Machynlleth, but they are not life histories or "truths" about us, or Machynlleth, or indeed research; they are about, as Speedy states, "moments and turning points in people's lives that they struggle to make sense of" (Speedy 2007, 6). We, that is myself and the co-researchers who have worked at Listening Point, have chosen which stories to share so that readers may glimpse something of our lived experience from these richer fuller descriptions of the project called Listening Point. The narrative is presented as a tapestry of voices that I hope can challenge the privilege of academic knowledge and also capture the experience of the research process (and life) itself, which is very rarely linear, often messy, and includes episodes of conversation, interaction with others, personal reflection, study/work and rest.

Within the research process of any therapeutic endeavour there are always questions of "power": who are the researched and who are the researchers? I wanted to ensure that the power differential between the researcher and the researched was minimal and transparent. As Speedy and Wyatt surmise:

> Collaborative approaches to research are of benefit to the practitioner (and other co-researchers) because they work explicitly and consciously with the expressions of power between people, exposing and challenging the dominant paradigm and opening up its assumptions – e.g. that professionals are the only sort of experts, and only professionals can be researchers to the investigation. Collaborative research, and specifically collaborative writing, can be seen as a reciprocal process through which each party generates and shares learning, for the purpose of creating knowledge for beneficial effect, and promoting voices that might otherwise be silenced (Speedy and Wyatt 2014b, 162).

The researchers' narrative will also be documented in this book, as the process was a transformational journey, a final act in our work together. Sometimes we met and our conversations triggered stories that we recorded and then transcribed; at other times we circulated chapter headings or other co-researchers' stories triggered further stories via email: For example, Lisa writes of a meeting and exchange of chapter outlines:

> It was so lovely to catch up with you and the group last week. It always feels special when we all gather around the teapot!
>
> Just a few paragraphs seem to jump from the headings for chapter 5 to 7.

She goes on to produce the contribution you will find in chapter 5.

Research conversations February 2014

Our conversations also "checked out" that the research process was on target and, indeed, contributed to the narrative account:

> *Sue: The first part of the book has been about the bad bits in a way, it has been about the search for April, the chaos, the stuff that was going on.*
>
> *The missing and the searching – always people here.*
>
> Lisa: You just got used to it really;
> the cafés were always full of chaps with dogs.

It just became part of life;
seeing the people on the hills.

Sue: I have been immersed in the writing, and away from Machynlleth. It felt a bit strange coming back today and seeing the hills quiet and sunny without any people on them.

So, are you feeling ok about what we're writing and how you are contributing?

Ceri: It's interesting isn't it that it's ok to think and feel now, that maybe I wouldn't have allowed myself to feel and think then.
A couple of times I have bumped into Maria and talked about that.
It's like another layer.
The word that came about a lot within our writing
was the word "surreal".
And that feeling about that at the time; it "was surreal".
How can you take it in properly if it is surreal?
Because your brain...
It feels like "I am trapped in a nightmare or a TV drama."

Sue: Perhaps it's a bit like trauma; you can't make sense of it so you detach.

Hope: Like an observer, a detached observer.
The shock of it.

Sue: My protection, I suppose, is that I dissociate.
I'm quite good at it!
I just switch off.

Ceri: I could have won prizes for dissociation!

Lisa: It's good if you can though.

Sue: Not always. Sometimes you do it when you don't want to and that can be really frustrating and upsetting because you can't feel joyful or "feel" the exciting things.

Hope: Yes. It can be quite difficult.

Sue: I am better now at having control over it I think.

Hope: I am just thinking about control,
and how nice it is to have a chapter at a time;
so nice and manageable.
Because when I think about the things that I have read,
and the things you have written,
I think,
"It is just in that chapter."
It is boundaried and manageable for me.
Although within the stories,
they are really upsetting,
I can manage it because...

What I feel is very comforting, is your
"padding it all out" in some way.
You are framing these painful stories with your words,
and your research,
And that seems to help me to be calmer about it.

Etherington describes her narrative research with ex-clients as an extension of the therapeutic process (Etherington 2001). One of my own ex-clients, Alex, who undertook a collaborative research project with me, takes this further:

> It's like the writing down of it in the research was the next stage of therapy on from the counselling. Different, yet so powerful. Each time I tell the stories they change and become less powerful in the "hurting" but more powerful in the "understanding". (Dale 2010, 62)

Lisa comments that by having the story a chapter at a time it feels "safer" and "less chaotic". Anne Marie compares this with her experience of the events as they unfolded when April went missing:

Anne Marie: I was just thinking about what you were saying about the chapter being boundaried and contained and also your own experiences of disassociation when that happened.

My experience of the search period though was not at all disassociated,

I couldn't get rid of it.
I couldn't escape from it.
I couldn't sleep,
I couldn't think.
I was physically in it all the time as my home
(in the centre of town)
and my office
(which was in the same building as the police command centre)
were where they were.

I was absolutely surrounded by the media and the police,
It feels now,
like a really contained period of time.

The search was six or seven months wasn't it?
It was such a long process.

Lisa: Yes, it was so long because first the trial was going to be at the end of February.

Then it was delayed.

Sue: My experience of writing the first chapters, however, was not at all contained, safe or boundaried.

It is interesting that Hope feels the chapters are quite contained.
When I wrote the first two chapters…
They were so chaotic;
fragmented,
I couldn't thread them together…
Perhaps this was because my memory of the time was so dissociated?
Kim Etherington, my supervisor, read the early versions and also commented that it was very fragmented.

It was not then so held, not so contained for me.
Whereas this chapter,
it feels a bit better.
It flows better.

Hope: That's very interesting.
When I think how I write about that time...
It's almost as if I could write it in bullet points rather than flowing.
Just a list of bullet points.

Sue: You'll see I have put your writing into poetic form,
This is how it felt to me.
I suppose more poetry rather than bullet points.

We then go on to discuss further how I will use the stories, and how they will be able to edit, amend, or delete their contributions as the process progresses. I discovered that when I asked for a contribution about a particular topic or chapter I often got stories that went backwards and forwards across time, covering periods that had already been written, which led to many drafts and versions of each chapter.

Sue: You might find that I have not used all of the stories you have sent as yet.

This is because they flow across different times, so I am using bits across the timeline of the book.

Lisa: The stories change as we tell them.
We are remembering more and more of the detail,
the funny bits and the really difficult bits.
I am noticing though that it is difficult to pin them down.

This ties in with the narrative therapy practice of re-authoring, when people are encouraged to re-tell their lives so that they become "richer thicker" descriptions of their lived experience (White and Epston 1990). This does not necessarily mean that the pain gets less but, as Sarah, one of my former counselling clients, told me, "it consumes me less, or more of me develops to support the pain and live" (Dale 2008, 76).

The other thing that seemed important to explore in the research was the extent to which our location and Welsh culture affected, or did not affect, how the events unfolded in Machynlleth. The first step in addressing this issue was to consider both the research from other communities coping with a traumatic event, and my own assumptions of shared identity with those around me.

Assumptions of shared identity

When we move into a community that seems to share a culture similar to our own, we can sometimes be fooled into thinking that we have a shared cultural identity. I had never thought of myself as anything other than "British". We had moved to Machynlleth, a town we knew well from our frequent holidays here, when my husband retired. I had worked there, as a psychotherapist in private practice, from a central consulting room, for three years.

When April was murdered, however, I felt very English amongst my very dear "Welsh" friends and colleagues.

Perhaps our cultural heritage and the histories that we re-enact through our telling of the stories of our shared past influence how we respond in the here and now?

Machynlleth is in the land of Owain Glyndwr, Celtic myth and the ancient site of the Welsh Parliament building. I remain aware that, within living memory, Welsh-speaking people were often not allowed to use their native tongue in churches and schools. I wonder what that must have felt like, to be forced to use the oppressor's language as your main means of communication?

Gallant speaks of the bullying his daughter experienced at school when he and his family moved to Shetland. Watching a reconstruction of an ancient Viking ceremony highlighted for him the great difference between the cultural history of Shetland and his own. He writes:

> We had presumed to step onto this foreign ground in the expectation that, like Earl Rognvald, Shetland would welcome us. Of course many did. And yet the morning wait for the bus was a scary schooling in how children search for self-identity and meaning (Gallant 2014, 72).

I had been and remained (but now consciously) an incomer in Wales. My cultural heritage is from the flat lands of Suffolk, where my ancestors gathered on the verdant Anglo plains and succumbed to the invading Roman legions.

Where the narratives are located and the cultural identity of those who feature in those narratives seem key elements in how any new community's (socially constructed) identity is formed (Sarbin 2005).

Some of the contributors to this book are people who have lived in Machynlleth all their lives, and some of us are incomers. I notice, however, that the book, and our conversations, are in English, and wonder what this means – or if it is even important.

Conclusions and considerations

This chapter has given a snapshot of the emerging research process and the way in which the emerging stories have been woven together to form a narrative account of a specific time in history in which we were all involved. It has also discussed how cultural identity may have influenced both our experience of the events and also the research process itself.

Padraig Ò Tuama, writing of his work with communities of reconciliation in Northern Ireland, advises:

> To tell a story means to see wisely. It is wise to speak of grief. It is wise to not rush hope. It is wise to not end a story before it is ended. It is wise to listen. It is wise to see (Ò Tuama 2014, 38).

I hope that, through the narrative research process, through this speaking of grief and the listening to others, we co-researchers and you, the readers of this book, will see more clearly.

CHAPTER FIVE

THE LISTENING POINT IS BORN

Sue's journal: December 2012

Christmas is approaching. I dread the thought of it.
How can we celebrate the miracle of life in the face of
what is happening here?
People hurry and scurry about, heads down.
Ashamed to be buying a gift for a child when another family has
lost so much.
Client referrals have increased, anxiety and depression increasing.
I am fielding the referrals. I find myself, unusually,
not wanting to see any clients at the moment.

Community update December 2012

12th December 2012
Coral and Paul Jones issue a heartfelt statement, 10 weeks after April's disappearance.

"The empathy shown towards us by not only local people but those from afar has shown us that people really do come together during difficult times," they say.

"We understand that Christmas will be a particularly difficult time without April being amongst us but as parents we will obviously acknowledge the festive season as best as we can." (BBC News at Six)

The search goes on

As December 2012 approached we were busy preparing to open the Listening Point drop-in before Christmas. We all recognised that such a family-orientated festival was going to be difficult, not just for those intimately involved, such as April's family, but for others as well.

How could people in Machynlleth celebrate when there was so much evidence of distress, and in the midst of the increased police activity? Police and specialist teams continued to scour the hillside, river, streams, people's outbuildings and even gardens and septic tanks.

There was discussion in the community about whether it was appropriate to put up the traditional Christmas lights in the town. A compromise was eventually agreed, Lisa remembers:

> The Christmas decorations began to be put up in Machynlleth, a special pink star and the town clock was flooded with pink light for the little girl who did not seem to come home. Machynlleth seemed suspended in a time warp.

Sometimes our own personal experiences and family crises added to our feeling that we were living in a parallel universe. When, as previously described, Ceri's partner became unwell and was rushed to hospital by helicopter:

> … there were people on the bridge and everywhere searching, and when the ambulance came for him there was this whole thing about a police escort and he went off in a helicopter.
>
> All the press were there because they thought it was something to do with the search and – getting all mixed up.
>
> Then later these policemen came into the garden… it is all surreal… I was well dissociated and it felt like I had been banged round the head.
>
> What actually happened was that I was in the house after the helicopter left and a friend was with me; he was telling me exactly what to do like "Put your shoes on, Ceri;" whatever he told me to do, I did.
>
> I was upstairs and heard him answer the door and came down. He was talking to some people in the garden and I was thinking, "Why are these people in the garden?"

They wanted to search the pond in the garden and of course the pond is "my pond".

Just the garden pond; I see it every day; it is just an ordinary pond. They looked at it and asked how deep was it. I said, "Well it will come up to your knees if you go in it, but you can walk around in it."

They said, "We will have to come back tomorrow with the diver," and I just burst out laughing because that was my garden pond... not deep enough for a diver... But actually the next day they came back and they had three people and they were walking the pond: one guy walked up and down, up and down, someone held him the whole time. And of course this seemed quite bizarre, but they were so tired... They had been everywhere, and searching everywhere, absolutely everywhere. His toes were touching every single part of the bottom of that pond. One guy was watching. It was so labour intensive, but it was completely bizarre because... that was MY garden pond. Just my garden pond.

But of course they were searching it because I live near the river.

Sue: The two situations were totally out of the ordinary, and traumatic, which made everything feel surreal?

Ceri: I suppose that whenever things happen in communities it would be very rare if we had nothing going on in our own lives – a good thing, or a bad thing, just something that keeps our mind occupied, and how bizarre that is. And that gets caught up together, so when I am writing about the situation in Machynlleth I've got these other things running along as well.

Sue: So you have a thread of this, and other threads of that, and together they are bizarre.

So it was against this backdrop of surreal events happening around us and events in our own personal lives that were sometimes challenging that we were making preparations to open the drop-in centre. We were very aware that we were "of the community" and affected by the issues, as well as "for the community" in that we were taking a stand and offering a small thread of hope in the form of hospitality, acceptance and welcome to those around us. The drop-in was not a place where "therapy" was prescribed, but it was set up intentionally with therapeutic values in mind.

The drop-in

We decided to open the drop-in two afternoons a week, on Wednesdays and Saturdays, and arranged a rota of volunteers to support the two experienced counsellors, one of whom would be at the drop-in. The volunteer counsellors (including me) also staffed the helpline. Helpline calls came through to a mobile phone, which we passed between us. We would have liked to open the drop-in for an evening session (which would have been more accessible to people who had jobs) but we had to compromise so that our volunteers were not over-stretched.

As stated earlier, we met together even when we did not have any visitors, to offer a visible alternative to the predominating narrative of "tragedy" playing out around us. It was important to avoid becoming trapped in the role of "rescuers" in what Karpman describes as a "drama triangle" (Karpman 2010).

Karpman developed the concept of the "drama triangle" to show dysfunctional social interaction. He likened these particular interactions to those seen in fairy stories where the damsel is always rescued from the wicked witch by the handsome prince, and then they live happily ever after. He writes: "A person 'living in a fairy tale' usually has a simplified view of the world with a minimum of three dramatic characters" (Karpman 2010, 2). Life, however, is much more complex than the simple fairy story; it is less stridently good and evil; it embraces a multitude of positions in between.

The three 'dramatic characters" within the fairy story and drama triangle are the victim, who is helpless and hopeless; the rescuer, who steps in to offer magical solutions for the victim, and the persecutor, who blames the victim and criticises the rescuer in their attempts to help.

All three characters can change roles when they are not satisfied by the outcomes of the interaction. For example, the victim can start to blame the rescuer for not supplying a good enough solution; the rescuer may start to blame the victim for not being "sad" enough, or not behaving as he or she imagines the victim should; the persecutor can move into the role of the rescuer by offering alternative solutions.

In Machynlleth the media were portraying what was happening as a story of "great evil": April and her family were the "tragic" victims; the "community" had the role of rescuer. The danger was that we in the community would be stuck with a role that would be impossible to fulfil: however much we wanted to, we could never bring April back or comfort the grieving family enough. We weren't even a single, heroic entity that thought or felt the same.

It would not have been effective for the Listening Point to have stepped into the "tragedy" story in a "rescuer" role. We wanted to help, but our intervention needed to stand outside the drama played out in the media's fairy story; it had to be able to encompass all shades and kinds of ordinary human needs and experiences. We had no magical powers; indeed, our "ordinariness", which left us at times feeling "so helpless" (as one volunteer put it), was often our strength. We were asked to support a multitude of activities – some practical, some mundane obtaining gravel for the residents making April's Garden, finding stones for the children to paint, making cakes for an event.

Interestingly, most of the time the atmosphere was light hearted. We discussed this during one of our research meetings.

Sue: Our kind of response to what was going on around us was to meet together and drink tea!

Ceri: And eat cake (laughter)!

Sue: It was a bit like setting up your stand and saying – this is normality in here, what is going on out there is madness. An alternative world if you like.

Lisa: And we were inviting others to step into that if they so wished;
to get out of the craziness for a bit.

Sue: I don't know what it was about being there that helped.

Lisa: It was something steady, something solid.

Others in the back of their minds knew there was a group of people there that they could go to; would always be available to listen or talk.
It was like a back-up, should they fall and need it.

Hope: In some ways though I thought
it was a back-up for me.
All of that was an added extra!

Lisa: I think we all felt like that too.

Hope: That was my coping strategy.

Sue: I realise now when I look back on it that I don't think I would have survived in Mach without that. Without you. Just being accepted and sitting…

It did feel different, though, because I was responsible for it,
and that felt big sometimes.
The images blur together;
the knitting, the stories from days gone by…
It felt like this little thread of something that wasn't bad.
Something that was really *good.*

Hope: Almost like rituals we were going through, and it makes me think about how people in other countries grieve.
I wonder whether we were doing a similar kind of thing?
We were grieving and going through a ritual; and it was about cake, and tea, and being together.

Different cultural rituals are found across the world that are helpful to people who have been traumatised. As van der Kolk and colleagues comment, "They are a very important part of the recovery from trauma;" they also need to be "sensitively acknowledged and respected as they enable survivors of trauma to re-engage with normal life" (van der Kolk, McFarlane, and Weisaeth 1996, 148). Our ritual, in true British style, was drinking tea.

Sue: And we are still sitting around with tea – no cake though (much laughter)!

Hope: The regularity, the knowing what will happen. The consistency was really important.
Even the laughter somehow.

Ceri: We were very light hearted most of the time.

Sue: And the relief of that.

Lisa remembers:

We opened our doors in the parish office in December and duly set about trying to make the room as welcoming and comfortable as possible, as it was slightly dark and gloomy. We kept all our equipment in the cellar as the room was used to hold parish meetings and various activities. We set out tables and chairs, taking care how they were arranged, as we didn't want whoever walked through the door to feel intimidated in anyway, or as though they were about to be put through an interview style situation.

We used tablecloths and put small vases of flowers on each table. We laid out games, puzzles, books and craft items, including a soft play area for children. A very large urn was on the go continually, which used to hiss and hum away in readiness to make vast quantities of tea and coffee. Cake and biscuits always seemed to be around, as well as around our waistlines as time went on!!

We played soft music in the background, so it would not feel like people were listening into conversations at another table. We organised a system of welcoming anybody who popped in, so turns were taken, rather than overwhelming people. We had the use of the back room if anybody needed a little privacy, as long as the vicar was not there, as this was her office.

We displayed a board outside offering a cuppa and a chat for anybody who so wished. We had some leaflets printed and delivered them around to various venues, to get the word around we were there if anybody needed us.

Initially all of us were volunteers. However we soon had enough funding to cover the costs of travel, and supervision (both for the drop-in volunteers and the counsellors) and to pay for a very small amount of administration support. It felt very important that the project should not be run by people who were "employed" to "help"; rather, it should be run professionally by, and for, people who lived in the community.

In retrospect, though, I wonder whether this was too idealistic – I found it personally very challenging to operate a professional service without attracting a professional persona; it was hard to remain just an ordinary member of the community, and I recognised that none of us involved in a professional capacity could go back to living as we had before October 2012.

The help-line

A new landline (initially at my house) was diverted to a mobile phone, which was passed between the three (later two) experienced counsellors. We opted to have an 0845 number, but most people phoned in on the landline number. As we were a charity, this telephone line was considered by the telecoms provider to be a "business line" and was also expensive in terms of line rental. It did, however, provide a vital link for people (especially those living in the surrounding villages) to talk about their hopes and fears. It was spasmodically busy, depending on what was happening in the community and being reported in media (see appendix 1 for statistics). The busiest time was during the trial, when many phoned in, both from the local community and further afield.

People phoned to get updates on what was happening in the police search, to find out when the drop-in was open, for "one off" counselling support sessions, for referral to ongoing counselling or volunteer contact, and we even had one person from outside the area who was lonely and isolated and who phoned regularly because they "needed to talk with someone who would listen". From time to time we also had the press using the number to ask for information about the project.

Counselling support

The experienced counsellors who staffed the telephone helpline were also available at the drop-in to support the volunteer listeners. We also provided one-off counselling sessions and assessments when needed.

However we decided it was not appropriate for the counsellors to formally counsel the volunteers or the visitors to the drop-in centre. Initially people who needed counselling were referred to a number of private counselling practitioners in the area, who had kindly agreed to donate some sessions on a voluntary basis, and to Cruse Powys and local drug and alcohol projects.

Counselling was seen as important for people who had specific issues that would benefit from a programme of sessions but we did not consider it necessarily the right response to a crisis situation when re-engagement with other members of the community might be more helpful. However, concurrently with the opening of the drop-in we began recruiting volunteer counsellors who would be managed directly by the project and would take referrals from the drop-in centre, the helpline and GPs, and self-referrals (see more on this in Chapter 8).

Conclusions and considerations

The model of having three levels of service was very successful but was used differently than we anticipated. I had assumed that the helpline and drop-in would be very busy and we would have only occasional counselling referrals. In practice, however, the helpline was indeed spasmodically busy, usually at key points in the police investigation when new facts were released into the public domain, and during the trial, or when someone wanted a counselling referral. The counselling service was slow to get started, and was accessed predominantly by people who lived outside Machynlleth; many referrals were, however, from the villages and hamlets surrounding the town, including the small village of Ceinws, where Mark Bridger had lived.

Similarly, the drop-in was only spasmodically busy: it was used by just two or three regular visitors, with more visitors at times of particular police or press activity. Many people dropped in to bring us offerings of cakes, plants and books, and then stayed for tea and to talk. These included community police officers, volunteers and clergy. It often seemed that people preferred to bring cakes and offers of help rather than be helped.

Several counselling referrals from the town's residents were seen by other agencies or private practitioners offering sessions on our behalf. The counselling service also remained well used in the year following the end of the trial and the funeral, whereas the numbers attending the drop-in reduced to one or two regular visitors.

Many local people who did not attend the drop-in, counselling service or use the helpline made it clear that they valued the service. There seemed to be something very important about our just "being there" and "being a safe place" that was visible within the heart of the community. As one man said, "I am so glad you are there. Knowing you are there and that I can come, or ring, means everything."

CHAPTER SIX

CHANGING LEADERSHIP

Sue's journal: February 2013

The pressure mounts as the trial approaches – it feels tangibly different in town as 25th February (the date set for it to start) approaches.

I am torn between the project running safely in Machynlleth, and being with my son who is seriously ill in Kettering. Surely things will improve?

The strain of "holding" everything together is making all of us at Listening Point look tired and there is a nervous restlessness that means we cannot quite settle to anything. I feel afraid as the trial approaches. I pray that Mark Bridger will plead guilty.

Community Update February 2013

19th February 2013
18:00 April Jones' parents are thought to be planning to attend the trial of Mark Bridger, which is due to start 25.2.13 at Mold Crown Court. (Sky News)

25th February 2013
Mark Bridger was arrested the day after the schoolgirl vanished while playing on her bike near her home in Machynlleth, Mid Wales, on October 1 last year. The 47-year-old was due to go on trial at Mold Crown Court today. But the case was adjourned by Mr Justice Griffith-Williams on application of the defence "to make further inquiries". (Daily Record).

Machynlleth had been bracing itself for the trial, which was expected to start on 25th February 2013. April's parents had decided to attend in person. The adjournment came as a surprise to most of us, and there was much speculation as to the reasons. Reporters in Machynlleth were soon asking "What do you feel about the trial being adjourned?" of anyone who would answer. More visitors used the drop-in centre and we wondered whether the venue was still suitable for a project that, it had become apparent, would continue longer than we had anticipated.

Changes in project leadership

February 2013 also brought changes to the Listening Point, which had now been running for two months.

As the weeks of the project turned into months, the two experienced counsellors who had helped set up the project recognised that it was more time consuming than they had expected; they were having to forsake other commitments and activities, and in February 2013 they decided to withdraw. Although we accepted their reasons it came as a shock, and I recognised that relying on experts to contribute their time in a voluntary capacity had its drawbacks.

We discuss their leaving at one of our research meetings:

Lisa: I remember when they announced they were leaving.
I remember thinking:
"You can't... you can't."
You can't just abandon us.
It was not much notice, it was just "We are going today and we are finishing."

Hope: Why did they go?

Lisa: Well I think they needed to get on and do their other stuff.

They felt they had done what they thought was helpful to set it up.

Sue: Perhaps the project was much bigger...
And much more difficult...
It was much more of a commitment than they thought it would be.
I felt sad.
They did not give me any notice.
I did not know until that moment when they said it in the meeting.
Because we had set this project up, and I could see it was huge, and then you have suddenly have two people who are the most

experienced leaving... I understood their reasons and respected them, but the little girl in me was saying, "But you can't leave me, Mummy."

Ceri: We nearly fell off our chairs.

Hope: I'm not surprised.

Anne Marie: It reminds me of that almost "suicidal" response you sometimes get with clients who can't cope with the process. And then they leave the counselling group or whatever.

Sue: It did feel a bit like that.

Lisa: They said, "You don't need us any more, you're all absolutely fine." And the panic – "I think we do, I think we do" (laughter).

Ceri: We couldn't say so at the time because we were so shocked.

Sue: I was shocked too.
I think in the meeting I just froze, I dissociated so that I could continue being the "professional" and hold it together somehow.

Anne Marie: Why didn't they talk to you?

Sue: I don't know. I think perhaps they thought if they talked to me they would end up staying.

It was the same week my son was diagnosed with acute renal failure, so I was not in a good place.

It was not a good week, that week.

I remember saying, after they had left, "We will never give up." We had a group hug.

Lisa: It felt a bit like... How many more kicks do you want?

Hope: But they did it anyway.

Sue: I think they could not face having that conversation really. I have seen them since, but we have never talked about why.

Hope: They had set up all sorts of counselling organisations in the past.

Sue: It is strange because, however tough it was at Listening Point, even though I was also a volunteer, I don't think I ever wanted to run off. Well, perhaps... but not in that sense... at least not 'til much later when I took a job on in England (laughter).

Lisa: I couldn't exit like that and just leave. It would have to have been a lot more slow and gradual. You did it in a very slow and prepared way. They just went.

Ceri: Then you came, Hope.

Lisa: It feels like you have always been there, from the beginning, though.

Hope: Yes, I popped in and said, "Hello, I'm here."

But I don't feel like I have always been here from the beginning;
beginnings are important,
and I wasn't here at the beginning,

I came later. Anne Marie came in later too, didn't you?

Anne Marie: Yes; much, much later, because I was working with the kids in parallel. Well, I didn't start working with the kids until the June.

Volunteering in a professional role

This change of leadership was pivotal, I believe, in the direction the project took after recovering from the shock of losing two such key figures. I re-evaluated how much could be expected of the volunteers. I recognised that it was perhaps not reasonable to expect other professionals to put their priorities on one side and give of their time, as I was currently able to do.

The profession of counselling emerged in the latter part of the 20th century and was mostly undertaken by those engaged in pastoral work in the voluntary sectors. People who were already working pastorally, as I was, undertook additional training to enable us to work better with clients who were presenting with depression, anxiety and many other mental health issues. In the 1980s or even early 1990s it was not seen as a "career" in the way that it is today. Over the years, however, the training and the expectations of counsellors have been professionalised. Professional standards have been introduced, in the form of a voluntary register, accreditation, ethical frameworks, and training standards to ensure practitioners are equipped to practise professionally, ethically and legally, in line with the other professions. What has not changed, however, is the lack of funded posts and the expectation that practitioners undertake voluntary placements. Also, the general public have become accustomed to receiving counselling freely on demand from GP practices and charities.

Counselling is an extremely skilled occupation, however. The training is expensive, supervision costly, and practitioners may hold high levels of responsibility in terms of safeguarding and working within the legal frameworks.

Over the last few years the question of whether counsellors should ever work unpaid has become one of the most highly debated issues in the profession. Hewett states a widely shared view:

> Counsellors are their own worst enemies as there is a fixation with voluntary work. One of my tutors on my degree course (who even taught the session on building a business) had never charged for counselling in her life. Volunteering as a student to build your required hours is fine, but why should we give away our hard-earned skills when no other profession has this built-in ethos? It destroys the market and perpetuates the "do-gooder" image (Hewett 2015).

Whether it is ethical to promote so many counselling courses (which students have to self-fund) and encourage students to expect to be entering a profession where they can earn a living (when there are very few paid counselling posts) is not a discussion for this book. However, I am mindful of the debate, and consider that volunteering is a valuable and healthy way for communities to support one another.

I was also conscious that the routine administration and running of the project was becoming more complex and there was a danger that we would not be able to "keep appropriate records" as required by the BACP Ethical Framework (BACP 2013). Although in theory it seemed appropriate for us all to be "volunteers together", in practice it was far more challenging.

As one of the volunteers commented, however:

> If we changed to a service run by "external experts" it would have changed how we were perceived by the community around us, and also how much the volunteers would have remained involved.

It was a difficult balancing act: having enough professional input so that the project operated safely and volunteers were not overloaded, and not asking more of volunteers than they had the ability and capacity to give.

One of the volunteer listeners agreed to take on a few hours of paid administrative work, freeing me to concentrate on taking an overview of the project, rather than the day-to-day management of the volunteer rotas. The remuneration she received was in no way adequate for the time she gave, over and above her contracted hours, and the skill with which she undertook the work, but it was, I hoped, a token of respect.

Supervision

For a counsellor, supervision is a professional requirement and an obligation and, I feel, an integral part of how the practitioner works within the therapeutic space. Supervision enables me as a practitioner to ensure that I am working in the best possible way with my clients. Many things can impede the therapeutic process: my own personal baggage, my level of skill and training, my prejudices, and even my physical health or my persona. My supervisor's role is to provide, as Gaie Houston puts it, "super-vision" (Houston 1990; Hewett 2015): a relationship that supports the counsellor by applying "super-vision" to the therapeutic process and where I, the counsellor, am within the field of therapy; a relationship that supports and challenges me as I process the stories clients have told me, helping me to deal with my own thoughts and feelings in relation to those stories. I like what Carroll (citing Ryan) says about it: "Supervision interrupts practice. It wakes us up to what we are doing" (Carroll 2011).

In the drop-in the remit was different from that of traditional counselling, but the stories heard were no less difficult to process. The volunteers did not come from a counselling background, so were not used to attending supervision; also they were not formally counselling clients; they were listening to visitors.

I had always thought that it would be helpful to provide a safe space, facilitated by an experienced counsellor/supervisor, where volunteers could "wake up" to what we were doing in the drop-in. These sessions would give them the opportunity to "de-brief" or talk about how the project, or whatever else was going on around them, was affecting their lives. As my role was more of a manager, the other two experienced counsellors had taken on this role and had initially provided bi-weekly debriefing sessions.

Assessing the position after they left Listening Point, it seemed vital that I was not the only trained counsellor involved. As I was manager of the project it would, I considered, be inappropriate for me to also provide consultative clinical supervision to the volunteers.

BACP's Ethical Framework for the Counselling Professions points out that:

> Good supervision is much more than case management. It includes working in depth on the relationship between practitioner and client in order to work towards desired outcomes and positive effects. This requires adequate levels of privacy, safety and containment for the supervisee to undertake this work. Therefore a substantial part or preferably all of supervision needs to be independent of line management (BACP 2015).

Hope was one of the counsellors I supervised in my own private practice, and she lived relatively locally. Faced suddenly with the loss of expertise within the project, and now with enough funding to be able to pay for some "debriefing and supervision" for the volunteer listeners, I asked her if she would be interested in taking on the role.

I was aware that this might give me a "dual role" in relation to Hope. Managing the project and offering her clinical supervision for her work there seemed inappropriate (she might after all need to raise issues about the project, or me), so we decided that we should arrange external clinical supervision for her in relation to the "debriefing and supervision" of the volunteer listeners. I was also conscious that, by asking this of her, I could be crossing boundaries in our relationship. As a supervisor, it was not my normal practice to ask supervisees to undertake work in which I was actively involved, both because of the unequal power relationships in any supervisory relationship (Houston 1990), which would make it difficult for them to refuse, and also because it could lead to a different kind of relationship, which might possibly interfere with my supervision of their private practice.

I was also aware that, within the supervisory relationship the focus is always on both the supervisee (and his or her needs) and the client(s). Within the drop-in space, the focus of work was held between us: we shared our lives in this unique space and time. I was not sure how this would impact on Hope personally, and on us, as supervisor and supervisee.

These, however, were extraordinary circumstances, and there were few people living locally with the relevant expertise. I knew also that Hope was a very gifted practitioner who had worked in many settings and felt she would work well with the group of volunteers. I was delighted when she agreed.

Hope recalls:

My first few sessions at the drop-in were quietly anxiety provoking, as it was already an established group and had been very ably supported by two very experienced counsellors, as well as Sue. It took me time to get to know everyone and let them get to know me. I feel this is a never-ending process: the safer I feel and the more understanding I have about myself, the more I feel I can share of myself with the group. If I am honest, I think writing this is also part of that process and has a very liberating feel to it for me. I feel the drop-in evolved: it twisted and turned in its own process, touching the people, not just in being there, but in providing a warm, safe space to come and a place to develop as a group, as an individual, as a community.

The levels here were deep and wide and, just as it stayed emotionally open, which I think encouraged a welcoming non-judging environment, I feel it started with a definite purpose and moulded itself to the responses of the people it served. Even though the project has finished, in some ways it is still not definitive; it is alive and well within the writing process.

The genuine kindness and warmth of the volunteers opened up an environment that in a "felt sense" seemed very congruent and in the moment. We laughed, we cried, we shared, we isolated; all was accepted, all was supported.

In a practical sense, it provided a centre or base that was grounded: a solid building with comfort and safety built in. I have seen from this place the branching out and touching of lives, if not directly, then symbolically in the being known about and staying omnipresent, ever-stable, true and sure. This is how it was in my life: a place to anchor my week; a reference point and means of feeling connected and settled. Perhaps for the first time in my life, I felt "This is a place I can belong, but in my own particular way. A place I can get to know others in a gentle, bit-by-bit, risking and withdrawing kind of way." This level is very sincere for me and fills a space inside unfilled before. I feel a shared connection of joy and pain of anger and confusion. The group itself is strong and robust and yet sensitive and gentle to its own and other's needs. I speak as if it lives as if it is a creature born from a tragedy and I think for me that is what it is. Perhaps a creature of a higher power – is this what can be created in the name of good, love and truth? I think for me it is and I am thankful for it.

Debriefing sessions continued and gradually changed from bi-weekly to a weekly "checking in" before the drop-in started – a group process. The volunteer listeners relaxed and enjoyed Hope's empathic "holding of the space". The sessions were a valued start to the week, and even described as a "lifeline" by some.

The volunteer counsellors and Hope and I also received independent supervision, which I am sure enhanced our practice and kept us working safely.

Delays in the legal process

The police team had informed me that the trial was planned to start on 25th February and was expected to last for about six weeks. I had also been briefed about the profoundly shocking evidence that would emerge. It came as a shock to all (including some of the police teams) when this did not happen and there was an unexplained adjournment (later it transpired this was for psychiatric assessments).

In the weeks leading up to 25th February the press had been gathering in Machynlleth, and considerable tension built up as community members prepared themselves to discover more about what had happened to April. To me it felt like a simmering pot with the heat turned up. Searching had been scaled up, the media presence increased, as did anxiety for the witnesses. April's parents had taken the courageous decision to go to court; finding there was now to be a delay of at least six weeks must have been very difficult.

Sue's journal: 25 February 2013
A phone call from the police team. The trial has been adjourned. I cannot believe what I am hearing. My thoughts instantly turn to April's parents who have made the long trip to Mold to face the man accused of murdering their daughter.

There is a kind of flatness as I enter the drop-in centre. There has been so much anxiety and stress in the lead up to the trial. We have been bracing ourselves for painful revelations. But there is also an expectation that we might finally learn the truth. There are so many things we do not know about what happened that night. Now the lid has to be squeezed back on all the feelings. The press ask that question again: "How do you feel about the adjournment?" I do not respond; I feel exhausted and like sleeping for a week. Then there is the knowledge that, having summoned the energy to get to this day, now another six- week wait approaches.

At Listening Point we had already recognised that we were not in the best location to undertake a longer-term support project. The parish office had been an ideal short-term base, but was proving difficult in the longer term: we lacked space to provide individual counselling, and our occupation of the rooms for two afternoons a week meant the church was unable to use the space as they would normally. They usually ran a charity shop there from early spring through the summer and regular coffee mornings to raise money for some proposed building works.

Several alternatives had been suggested by the volunteers, but as yet we had not narrowed down the best options.

We felt that moving during the trial would not be an option. The delay to the trial was therefore in some ways fortuitous, in that it gave us time to explore alternatives; it also gave us something purposeful to do to fill those weeks.

A building owned by Powys County Council had become available on the Bryn-y-Gog estate. It was self-contained and had been many years previously a little shop serving the estate. In recent years the Council had used it to house a community project but this had now come to an end and the building had been vacated.

We applied to the Council (in accordance with its tendering policy) to use the space to house Listening Point for six months.

Considerations and conclusions

- Careful thought is needed as to how best to use volunteers and how much can reasonably be expected of them. It seemed vital in Machynlleth to get the balance right between professional and volunteer input, so that it remained a community-led initiative, rather than a service provided by experts.

- Another point worth considering is that most volunteers coming forward at a time of crisis do so because of an emotional response. They may not know what to expect if the project needs to be sustained over a long period of time.

- In Machynlleth we felt that independent supervision was essential to ensure both volunteer listeners and counsellors worked safely and appropriately. When budgeting for a new project it is important to consider the cost of providing supervision, as it is unlikely that a supervisor with appropriate qualifications and experience will be able to offer the service on a voluntary basis.

- The police investigation and court processes were complex and changed rapidly. Liaison with the police teams ensured that we could adapt the support we offered to meet changing community needs and that we could give feedback to and be respectful of the needs of April's family.

- It is worth remembering that police investigations and court proceedings can go on longer than expected – it is important to build in contingency plans in case of delays.

CHAPTER SEVEN

MOVING TO THE BRYN-Y-GOG ESTATE

Sue's journal: March 2013
We have been to see the "Old Shop" on the Bryn-y-Gog estate today. My first thoughts were, "I am not sure if this is the right thing to do." The concerns running through my mind are partly practical – can we afford it? Will it be too close to April's family? Other thoughts included whether I wanted to, or had the inner reserves to, keep going for another six months at this level of working. With my son so ill in Kettering, how do I manage and prioritise both? Saying yes to this is another layer of commitment.

Community Update March 2013

13th March 2013
"Controversy over 'pink bows' as local businesses ask for them to be removed as there is fear they will damage business." (Cambrian News)

The "Old Shop", had, in recent years, been used by a Council-funded initiative called Communities First. They helped small community groups with funding applications and other support for their projects. They had left the building, but had left behind all the office equipment (minus computers), such as filing cabinets, desks, office chairs, printers, paper, print cartridges and envelopes. It would have been ideal if we had wanted to run an office, but it was not so good for a relaxed drop-in and counselling centre.

When we initially viewed the building the metal shutters were drawn down, so the building was dark and depressing. I wondered whether it was madness; opening this centre, here at the heart of the estate, would mean committing to a much longer project than I had first anticipated. I had naively assumed, when we opened the doors in December 2012, that the project would be completed within about six months (up until the trial had finished). The delay in the trial and the continuing stress for the Machynlleth community meant that our planned six months was now looking more like 12 months.

Having discussed it with the volunteers and the trustees of our hosting body CCSW, I (via the police family liaison officers) asked April's parents and other local community leaders what they thought; the response was resoundingly affirmative.

Powys Council offered us a six-month lease for a peppercorn rent and, on a rather gloomy day at the end of March 2013, we were given the keys.

All the office equipment and furniture had been left for our use and this posed a problem, given what we wanted to do. But nothing was going to deter the volunteers. The large desks and filing cabinets were stored by the Town Council; we then started the process of transforming the office into a more relaxed space.

Lisa writes:

It became apparent that we would have to find an alternative place for the Listening Point project to be run from, as the church rooms were needed for other requirements. A Community First project had lost its funding; a building came available that had originally been the local shop on the same estate where April and her family lived.

Sue confronted us with the idea; would it work for us? Clearly there were a few reservations, first thoughts being, would it be too close to where April lived and disappeared? The premises overlooked the garden that was being established for little April. It was a short distance out of the town, therefore would it be convenient for most service users?

After visiting the building we knew it would be perfect. So, after much paperwork and official form filling, endured by Sue, we were offered the use of the building.

We were a little apprehensive also about how our presence might be interpreted on arrival (such as a bunch of middle-aged, middle-class, so called do-gooders!!!!) Thank goodness, I don't believe this was ever the case.

We hauled up the bags of equipment from the cellar one last time (amazing nobody ever fell down those steps!!) and transported everything to our new abode. We went about turning an office into a lovely sanctuary. There was a hive of activity and rushing around to gather any accessories we might be able to use, as the "open day" was just a few days away. We received donations from some of the people who dropped in to see us and I remember paying a visit to one of the many so-called antique shops in Mach and bartering with the owner for a rocking chair, to be used in our new, private little counselling room, to be filled with throws and soft cushions.

The building had previously been used as an office and a lot of equipment had been left behind, so we cleverly disguised much of this with bright tablecloths and put things to good use. It was beginning to take shape and look great.

The bonding of our unit of volunteers continued (greatly scaled down by now into a smaller band). It was very important that we were a solid body, showing a united front to those people who sought our help. It was very much a learning curve for us all as we tried to process and deal with our own emotions as individuals and as a group. It became apparent very quickly that a strong and growing support for each other was forming, as we shared our inner thoughts and feelings. A true sense of friendship was emerging.

The original date for the trial of Mark Bridger was February, but it had been postponed for the gathering of further evidence. The agonising waiting continued; people were left not knowing what to think; children were confused and frightened, as were their equally bewildered parents. Local schools made additional counselling provision for the children. Parents reported that some were afraid to go to sleep, let alone go out to play.

Waiting seemed to be the most difficult thing. Ruth Burgess, a resident of Dunblane and member of the Iona Community, sent us a prayer that really resonated and was copied onto notice boards and appeared in the local press.

In quiet and in sadness
we wait
with questions and anger
we wait
with friends and with family
we wait
we wait and we cry "How Long"?
in the morning and the evening
we wait
as the world goes on around us
we wait
with an emptiness inside us
we wait
we wait and we cry "How Long"?
with the town of Machynlleth
we wait
with our children and our neighbours
we wait
with all who are sad and exhausted
we wait
we wait and we cry "How Long"?
Ruth Burgess, November 2012 (reproduced with permission)

Living with "not knowing" what had happened and not being able to speak about our worst fears (as this felt very negative and disloyal to April's family) was dreadful.

Marion Partington, whose sister was murdered by Fred and Rosemary West, writes: "We had better not dare to rehearse that scene, because even putting it into words would be tempting fate" (Partington 2012, 23). She goes on to say:

> The whole of Not Knowing had its own drill-like momentum. It was becoming a deep pit, eroded by our not being able to share our feelings about it. The conspiracy of silence required a mutual adherence to an unspoken law. In our ignorant attempt to protect each other from pain, and deny our own feelings, we tried to carry on as if nothing had happened. We were becoming more isolated from each other (Partington 2012, 24).

CHAPTER EIGHT

SETTING UP A COUNSELLING SERVICE

Sue's journal: May 2013
The normally bustling drop-in centre is quiet today; it is one of the afternoons set apart for counselling. Maria makes me a cup of tea and welcomes the counsellor who arrives ready to see her clients and then, as the counsellor prepares, Maria sits with me at a table and we talk quietly.

Strangely I feel a longing for the safety of the counselling room, "the womb" as one of the clients refers to it, rather than my usual role here of holding the therapeutic space within the drop-in.

My training has ensured that for me, usually the counsellor, the counselling space is a safe space; the work is boundaried by time, walls, protocols and ethical frameworks. We contract how we will work together, where and when we will meet. I explain confidentiality, and those rare occasions where this may not be possible. The counselling hour comes and goes with a regularity that enables me to allow myself to touch the pain of the other person in the room. It allows me to reach out and enable exploration. Stories told in the counselling room stay there. When I leave the space only the echoes of the person, as someone who by their telling has changed me a little, come with me. The space is almost a "sacred space" that holds and absorbs all confidences. Usually only the client, I and my clinical supervisor (who oversees my work) know what is spoken about.

My experience of the drop-in is different. It is the same in that it allows what I see to be the linking of lives through story-telling, but it is not contained in the same way; it is somehow wild and vibrant. It has the therapeutic qualities and principles and is governed by the same ethical qualities, but it is less about withdrawing from the community to the privacy of one intimate relationship and more about bringing the intimate relationship into a community setting. It is about being visible, whereas counselling, and the counsellor, are often invisible. Sometimes the openness, the enormity of that, makes me feel a bit vulnerable. Is it possible to offer core conditions of empathy, unconditional positive regard and acceptance within a public setting? The vulnerability for me is perhaps about feeling exposed.

I talk about this with Maria, who is wise beyond measure. She tells me, "It is all about caring for other people, trying to help. When we are here together it is about all of us reaching out to that other person who has dared to step through the door."

Community update

27th March 2013
"The search for missing five-year-old April Jones is expected to end in a few weeks, says Dyfed-Powys Police.

- "Officers from around the UK have been searching for the five year old since she disappeared from near her home in Machynlleth, in October.

- "Searches of specific areas of land will continue but they are expected to be completed at the end of next month.

- "Mark Bridger, 47, denies abducting and murdering April as well as intending to pervert the course of justice.

- "He is due to stand trial at Mold Crown Court on 29 April.

- "April's disappearance has sparked one of the largest police searches in UK history." (www.bbc.co.uk/news)

Background

As previously mentioned, there were benefits in linking the Listening Point project to an existing charity with a track record in delivering counselling using volunteer counsellors in many locations across Wales; one was that we had a ready-made governance structure of protocols and procedures.

CCSW had, at that time, 26 counsellors of varying levels of experience who were attached to eight supervision groups across Wales. It had been delivering generic counselling for 17 years, initially to clergy of all denominations and more recently to adults in the general public in those areas where counsellors were available. The service was funded through a variety of sources, including the Church in Wales, the Welsh Presbyterian Church and the Welsh Government.

It is normal practice during counselling training for student counsellors to be asked to complete a counselling placement, and many voluntary organisations, including CCSW, recruited students engaged in diploma-level training and provided them with support, supervision and reports to their training institution. In exchange the trainee provided an agreed number of referrals or counselling hours per week.

The support and supervision CCSW gave to trainee counsellors was of a high standard, and I felt confident that counselling delivered was also of a high standard (this was reflected in client evaluations), so I was happy to adopt this governance for supporting volunteer counsellors at Listening Point.

In December 2012 we conducted interviews with a number of volunteer counsellors who were studying for a diploma in counselling at a local college.

The application process included completion of a comprehensive application form, two references (one of whom was the counsellor's tutor), an interview, and post-interview Disclosure and Barring Service (DBS)[2] checks. Competition was fierce (we had a good reputation for placements, and often courses recruit more students than there is available work).

We also recruited a new, experienced supervisor to work with the trainees. All of this took time, especially with regard to the DBS checks (which in our area took nine weeks from application to completion).

Practical considerations

In April 2013, the first counsellor started working from a counselling room in the new Listening Point building.

---

[2] More information can be found about the DBS (Disclosure and Barring Service) from their website: https://www.gov.uk/disclosure-barring-service-check/overview

To access the room set aside for counselling meant entering the building either through the back door or through the room used for the drop-in. In either case it would be apparent to those attending the drop-in or passers-by on the estate that the counselling room was in use. We were mindful that people accessing the counselling might not feel comfortable with this, and it would be difficult to maintain client confidentiality. Also, if we ran the counselling sessions concurrently with the drop-in, then we would be unable to use it if needed for someone accessing the drop-in. We decided therefore to offer counselling on days when the drop-in did not operate. This was, however, sometimes challenging in that, when we opened up the building and switched lights on, local people noticed and dropped in to see us, even if it wasn't a drop-in day. On the whole we managed this quite well and held the boundaries; gradually it was accepted that dropping in was only welcomed when the sign (which one of the volunteers designed) was outside, or the door was open.

We were also aware that some people found it difficult to come onto the estate where April had gone missing, and many found the sight of April's garden very emotional. When taking a referral I took care to say where the sessions would be held and if necessary we would refer people to an alternative local therapist.

Counselling records

In accordance with the BACP Ethical Framework (2013), we ensured that "adequate records" were kept. This included basic information such as the person's name, address, telephone number, and GP contact details. All clients were asked to sign a standard contract in accordance with CCSW policy. We also collected basic statistical data using CORE-IMS,[3] a widely used tool for measuring the effectiveness of therapy (see appendix 1 for a summary of the data).

Counselling delivery

Two of the counsellors on placement were trainees who were studying for an integrative diploma in counselling; the third was engaged in the final part of an integrative Buddhist psychotherapy diploma. All worked to the BACP Ethical Framework for Counsellors and Psychotherapists and

---

[3] For more information see the COREIMS website:
http://www.coreims.co.uk/About_Measurement_CORE_Tools.html

received supervision with experienced supervisors, in accordance with BACP recommended best practice (BACP 2015).

In total the counsellors delivered 129 sessions of counselling between April 2013 and July 2014 when the Listening Point ceased taking referrals in preparation for the project ending.

Client experience of Listening Point

Although no full accounts have been included within this publication about the experience of receiving counselling from the project, the following anonymised statements are some of those given to us in the counselling service evaluation forms.

"It was a lifeline, she was an amazingly good listener."

"Being here at the heart of where it all happened, and talking, helped a lot."

"It was an excellent and professional service."

"I feel I can go on with my life now."

"Having the opportunity to speak confidentially to someone who really listened made all the difference."

"The room felt like a womb, really safe."

"It was hard to come here, to this place, but I am very glad that I did."

"Thank you."

Volunteer counsellors' experience of Listening Point

Over the length of the project, three trainee counsellors on placement worked from the centre, and all of them successfully completed their training.

Mel writes of her time working at Listening Point:

My experience as a counsellor with the Listening Point is something that I will always cherish. As it was my first placement and being very inexperienced, the Listening Point gave me confidence in my practice. The people, both paid and volunteers, involved in the project were the most extraordinary I have ever met; from all walks of life, but all were the most welcoming people. From this the Listening Point always had a most welcoming atmosphere; it almost felt as if you were held – *cwtched* – by all who you met there, especially Maria who welcomed me each week. The way people interacted with each other with complete acceptance was felt by myself as well as the people who used the project. I was sad the project ended but so proud to have been a part of the Listening Point.

Above are the words that I have thought of, whilst sitting writing this, but I have just got my portfolio out and looked what I have written there. Here is a brief summary:

- A clear structure within the project
- Good support from Project Manager and Administrator
- Project Manager was very supportive and good at directing me to further research or information
- Regular training was offered and good induction.

I have enjoyed my placement at the Listening Point and it is a shame that it is closing, as I would have carried on counselling after I had completed the required 100 hours. This placement has given me the confidence to go forward. I felt that my opinions were counted as part of a team; I will miss this placement and team.

Hope and I also offered one-off counselling sessions, when needed, to those attending the drop-in who needed the privacy and space to talk through a specific issue on a one-to-one basis. We were also able to refer on people who had specialist needs to external agencies (such as local substance misuse service), school counselling, Cruse Powys and a number of local practitioners who were happy to support the project.

I also offered both one-off sessions and occasionally a series of sessions of telephone counselling to people unable to access the centre who self-referred via the helpline, and occasionally a series of face-to-face sessions when appropriate. I did not charge for these services, but included them within my private practice in terms of insurance, supervision and record keeping.

From time to time we also referred people back to their GP for referral for mental health assessments or if we felt they needed to be assessed in relation to medication or another medical or psychological intervention. Unfortunately, as discussed previously, the mental health provision in Powys was very poor, so it was very difficult to get follow-up support for anyone with an acute mental health disorder. On one occasion we were left for over five hours supporting a person experiencing an acute mental health crisis while waiting for an ambulance; there was no one from the GP practice or mental health team who was prepared or able to do an emergency mental health assessment. The only place of safety other than the A&E department at the hospital in Aberystwyth (which did not have any crisis mental health team available) was Aberystwyth Police Station; the paramedics opted to take him to the hospital, from where he was later discharged as there was no psychiatrist on duty to assess him. Fortunately his elderly parents were able to help keep him safe until the community mental health team arrived, 48 hours later.

I was shocked at the disparity of provision between "health-care" and "mental health care", and also very aware that it meant that the Listening Point was very vulnerable: we had no back up if one of our visitors or counselling clients experienced a deterioration in their mental health and we were concerned for their safety.

Considerations and conclusions

When considering whether to set up counselling provision in the context of a crisis support intervention, it would seem important that:

- someone suitably qualified (ideally an experienced, accredited practitioner and supervisor) manages the provision
- there is a clear system for the referral and allocation of clients to counsellors
- protocols and procedures are in covering the recruitment of counsellors, confidentiality, safeguarding, record keeping,

monitoring and supervision. This will protect both the counsellors and those accessing the service

- suitably qualified independent supervisors are contracted to provide clinical supervision, separate from the management of the project, to avoid dual roles, as recommended within the BACP Ethical Framework for the Counselling Professions

- careful attention is paid when assessing potential clients as to their suitability for counselling, and the location of that counselling. Ideally an initial assessment should be carried out by a senior practitioner

- the counselling is provided from suitable premises, ideally with other people working in the building, so the counsellor is not working on their own

- project managers know where to obtain support for clients of the service if their mental health deteriorates or medical intervention is needed. A clear referral pathway needs to be developed.

CHAPTER NINE

COMMUNITY FUN DAYS, BIRTHDAYS AND FIREWORKS

Sue's journal: April 2013
April 4th, I understand, ***is*** *(I still cannot bring myself to write "would have been") April's sixth birthday. I cannot imagine how that must be for April's family. I thought I was good at empathising, had learned all there was about allowing myself to resonate with the feelings of people in pain, but my mind just will not let me go there. I find myself doing mundane tasks, keeping busy – distractions, anything but the reality of murder and a body not found. I can understand the family's need to have an event; also other viewpoints voiced by members of the community who would not choose to remember in this so public a way.*

We will be there, though, to offer a little support... when what is probably needed is a miracle.

Community update April 2013

10th April 2013
"The search for missing five-year-old April Jones is expected to end in a few weeks, says Dyfed-Powys Police"

"Since last October, specialist officers along with other forces from across the UK have been searching the area in and around Machynlleth for April Jones."

"In a statement, Dyfed-Powys Police said:

'It has been a massive search operation where an area of 60 kilometres square has been searched including and have over 300 specific search areas.'

'The terrain is extremely challenging. The mountains, gorges, streams and waterfalls in the area mean extra care has to be taken and specialist safety equipment has to be worn.'

'The force made a commitment to search until all viable lines of enquiry were complete.'" (www.bbc.co.uk/news)

Community events

An important part of life in a rural community, especially one as vibrant as Machynlleth, are the events that regularly take place such as the town carnival, the comedy, art and music festivals, the bi-annual El-Sueno (Latin American Festival), the pantomime and the lantern procession, which starts with a lantern parade through the town followed by fireworks in the park. As the latter was due to take place at the end of October, it was the first event due to take place after April's abduction. The organisers were unsure what to do: whether to go ahead or cancel it. April's parents publicly affirmed that it should go ahead and children used their half-term holidays (as usual) to attend the lantern-making workshops.

Apart from an open day, which we hosted when moving to our new centre, all the events had their own organisers, although on occasions we were asked to assist with specific events, and chose to support all of them, and the people attending them (or in some cases finding them difficult to attend) as much as we could. I have only commented here on the lantern parade and the events that Listening Point was directly involved with. During this period event organisers liaised with the police and with April's parents to ensure that they respected Paul and Coral's wishes and did not compromise the police investigation and forthcoming trial.

It was interesting that, at all of the events, the lantern procession included, there seemed to be moments when everything was "normal" and just as it always had been – a momentary forgetting of the terrible events that had taken place – and then "jarring moments" when the reality of a child murdered and a massive police search were remembered. These moments generated a number of visible emotions: fear, anxiety and sometimes even anger. In the early days of the search, there were outpourings of support for the family, and also outpourings of grief, but as time passed the reactions from the wider community became more diverse and in some ways seemed more painful.

Van der Kolk and colleagues make the point that

> … often after the initial outpouring of community support begins to wane. This period of "disillusionment" can be characterised by negativism, scapegoating, disorganisation, withdrawal of support, and a full realisation of the extent of the trauma and loss (Van der Kolk, Mc Farlane and Weisaeth 1996, 465).

Citing Norris (1992), they go on to point out that "individual traumas present a greater public health challenge than disasters do" because they do not get the degree of acknowledgement and psychological support, even though the number of people affected by the incident(s) could be as great as in a major disaster (ibid, 465).

It is interesting that Mike North, commenting in relation to Dunblane and aspects of what he describes as "a public private grief", goes on to say:

> Somehow each one of us was going to have to find a way of achieving a balance between our own private grief and the reality of being part of a public tragedy. That would be all right if those promises of help for as long as we needed it were kept, and as long as the community could deal with the public aspects of the tragedy as well as the private grief. In particular, the people of the town must avoid thinking that it was unbecoming for the victims' families to say things in public and remind others about what happened (North 2000, location 1726).

Here in Machynlleth, April's family's personal grief was indeed made very public, and community members supporting them were also affected by varying degrees of trauma and bereavement. But I noticed that, while the community was supportive of the family in their personal grief, there were times when some found their public expression of it difficult to bear (especially as time went on).

Bereavement studies (Parkes and Prigerson 2010) tell us that each person grieves in a different way, with periods of sadness, anger, fear, anxiety, guilt, loneliness, and numbness, but not everyone experiences these feelings within the same timeframe or to the same level of intensity. Van der Kolk (1996) and colleagues point out that the feelings are far more pronounced when the loss is traumatic and disrupts familiar patterns. As discussed earlier, the media also have an impact and add a layer of stress. Events such as the Lantern Procession, April's birthday party and the "fun day" were broadcast across the world, and that in turn brought many visitors, who were at times very supportive but also made judgements about the behaviours and emotional responses of those intimately involved with the events.

Lantern Procession 2012

Both Maria and I were among the crowds (which included many police and media) on the streets at the Lantern Procession that year.

Sue's journal: November 2012
Last week was the annual Lantern Parade. I stood with others and watched as the eerie procession of enormous angels approached with the sound of music – a song composed for April. The children in the procession seem excited and happy. A child runs out from the crowd to join a friend, and a mother, with tears running down her face, clutches him back to her. The fear seems infectious; parents cling onto struggling children, lanterns in angel form guarded by police. I feel my heart will break. For the children, parents, and those many police on duty.

Maria writes:

One thing that has stuck in my mind is the Lantern Procession. The first one after the tragedy was bigger and better, as if everyone had decided to do something fun and exciting, and I remember standing watching it and thinking, "This is good, this is right, the children are happy." There were families involved, the mums and dads walking with their children in the procession. This stood out for me, as usually one parent would accompany the child and the other watch from the side with other, usually older, children; this time it was a family affair. There were a lot of angels made out of lanterns and I thought it would be helpful for the children to let them go or burn them at the end. The atmosphere was good, I was glad to see the police officers laughing and taking part in something nice.

Right at the end of the procession though, someone drove a car with a song written about April playing on a loudspeaker and the atmosphere changed immediately; people's conversations became all about what had happened and the mood was bleak once again.

A few days later I was having a haircut and my hairdresser, who has two young children, said that her kids had been having a great time until the car came past and they both started crying and wanted to go home. That night her little boy wet the bed, something he hadn't done for a long time, and she felt everything had been stirred up again, just when the children were moving on.

I was very concerned in the months following the murder that it must have been so difficult for school teachers and organisers of events such as the procession to somehow involve the family and acknowledge what had happened but at the same time protect all the other families and children, particularly those who had suffered tragedies in their own lives and may have been experiencing re-surfacing emotions because of this.

Celebrating a birthday

Following the adjournment of the court hearing at the end of February I was approached by the police family liaison officers to see whether volunteers from Listening Point would support April's family; they wanted to hold an event on the Bryn-y-Gog estate to commemorate what would have been April's sixth birthday. The intention was to organise something fun for the children who had been April's friends and neighbours and acknowledge in some way her loss. We were asked to make cupcakes (preferably with a pink theme) and help on the day. School children were asked to write messages for April, which were then tied to pink helium balloons. By the time we arrived on a cold, bright early April afternoon there were already hundreds inflated and ready for launch, and large trestle tables set up to receive cakes. This event was the subject of one of our research discussions.

As I listen back to our conversation, I become aware that in the listening, and the transcribing, of those words a different narrative emerges; different from the experience of talking together. It is, as Etherington puts it, a "reflection on reflections" (Etherington 2000, 13). The cadence and resonance of our voices take on the shape of poetry rather than prose. New truths emerge for me that were absent during our original conversation. I understand what Cixous and Calle-Gruber mean as they write, "What is most true is poetic. What is most true is naked life. I can only attain this mode of seeing with the aid of poetic writing" (Cixous and Calle-Gruber 1997, 4).

As I write in an earlier publication:

> If poetry is defined by rhythm, structure, resonance and is evocative and, as Bachelard (1964) points out, "exists in sound within its resonance and reverberation" (Bachelard cited in Behan 2003), conversation also has these qualities. We do not speak as we would write, and do not use the formal grammatical prose of written documents, but our words, as we speak them, are also defined by rhythm, structure and resonance. Especially, it seems, when we are speaking of things that are important to us. (Dale, 2008)

As Tedlock (1983) writes:

> If anthropologists, folklorists, linguists, and oral historians
> are interested in the full meaning
> of the spoken word
> then they must stop treating oral narratives as if
> they were reading prose
> when in fact they are listening to dramatic poetry.
> (Tedlock 1983, 123)

Here our reflections are included as a "collective biography" of the event rather than our individual memories. As Davies and Gannon note:

> We search for those "scenes, moments, illustrations" that take us to an unexpected wonderful place of resonance and agreement, not just among ourselves but with others who read what we finally write (Davies and Gannon 2006, 115; Davies et al. 2001).

Collective voice:
We had April's birthday party with all of those pink balloons.
I remember us all being frozen,
and all the cakes.
Yes all those cakes,
and it was so, so cold.
We were like blocks of ice and it was freezing;
and we were there for hours and hours.
It was sunny but so, so cold.
There was a determination in the air –
"We are going to see this out to the end."
Then there were all these cakes everywhere and I was thinking:
"But who is going to eat these cakes?"
It was not really a day to be standing round eating cakes outside.
But it was April's birthday.

April's parents wanted to have a birthday party
for the children on the Bryn-y-Gog.
It was April's birthday.

We were still running the drop-in from the Parish Office,
thinking about moving to this place,
this estate.
The police family liaison officers wanted desperately to do something,
anything, to help April's parents.
They knew it would be such a difficult day;
April's birthday.
April's parents needed to do something,
something that was going to be positive for the other children;
so they decided they would have a party for them.

We were asked whether we would make some cakes;
so we duly made cakes and went to support them.
Just like a village fete really.

April's parents had made a beautiful big cake.
We were invited into their house and I thought:
"Oh no, how did we end up in the house?"
It felt like, "This is an intrusion." I had no intention of going in.
We were invited to help blow up balloons.
I remember the room, so many balloons.
There was a need to keep April "out there" and be remembered.

I retreat when grieving, so it would not be my way.
But for some people it is very important;
they take comfort in having others around them.
Everyone deals with everything differently I suppose.

That is quite challenging for me.
It is not about right or wrong, it's just that when you talk about it –
I feel –
If it had been me as a parent,
I could not do that for me.
I couldn't have coped with that.

I remember that we were also eyeing up the building;
we were debating as to whether or not to take it on.
Is this too close?
Are we going to manage here?
The family were encouraging us to come.
I was looking at all the press and the people and thinking,
can we cope here?
You wanted to be there for solidarity with them,
even if it was not your way
exactly –
You want to stand alongside in some way.

For me the more you talk about it the more I just want to…
run away.
Makes me feel quite upset and angry.
Like, "get away."
It brings up quite a lot for me and I am quite surprised about it.

Quite a lot of negative feelings really.
And it is then so hard to empathise;
it's quite hard to detach myself from my feelings.
I quite understand, and of course it was right for them, but when it's not right for me I am quite surprised at
how powerful those feelings are
and those different needs could, I guess,
cause some conflict with others.

But the children seemed to enjoy it.
They sent their balloons up to April and children ate the cake.
One squashed a pink sticky one on his little sister's nose!
There was a lot of laughter
and tears.

It did not happen in the same way the following year.
Things had moved on.

And if it was good for the children then,
what happens, I wonder, afterwards, to the children?

It makes me think about the ribbons that were there for so long and then they are gone.

I remember singing the "Happy Birthday",
the pain of that
and the balloons sailing off into the air.

We're still talking about April, and those events,
but what about everyone else?
No one talks about it here now.
What's that like for the children I wonder?

When April first went missing waves of pink ribbons (pink being April's favourite colour) were tied around lamp posts, front doors and shop fronts and people wore them on their clothes as a mark of respect and to show solidarity with the family.

Ceri remembers, however, that:

The pink ribbons that were around all the lampposts and doors
But as time went on they split a lot of people, didn't they.
Some wanted them, some hated them; and that argument still goes on.
There are still ribbons in places, and also arguments.

Some people feel that it helps them to remember and that makes them feel better
and for others it makes them feel absolutely awful.
They just remember all the really awful things.

For me the pink balloon day was huge in connection with my personal life because January 3rd is a sad anniversary for me.

It was a lovely sunny day,
I went up there with the cakes. I asked myself,
"Why don't I feel anything?"
It was the press that I remember the most;
silent but waiting.
I hated the press waiting.

Like vultures.
Waiting for vulnerability.
For emotion on a face.
Why would anyone want a photo of the pain on your face?

When I went in the house to blow up the balloons I could feel an atmosphere in the house that I recognised, which I think of as "Angels".

It was like everything was so protected in the house and it felt like the police were doing that so well.

I thought that perhaps by going in we were helping to break up something of the pain, taking some of it away somehow?
I hope so anyway.

Because from my own experience sometimes the pain is so heavy and big
that you are burdened by it.
I hoped that people coming into the house might lighten it a bit.

I also remember with a smile that the kids were having fun.
Some of them were playing really inappropriate music loudly through ghetto blasters.
I was dancing myself that evening.
Thank God I was dancing.
I was ill the next day though.

Bryn-y-Gog Fun Day

Another event we were asked to help with was a Fun Day. This was organised and funded primarily by a local company who wanted to do something for the children of the Bryn-y-Gog. As we were by this time occupying the building on the green in the centre of the Bryn-y-Gog we found ourselves volunteering to both run a drop-in café serving tea, coffee and hot dogs and provide indoor creative play for children and a storyteller outside in a tent.

Lisa remembers:

A lovely idea to try and gather the broken community together for a little light-hearted fun and games for the children. There was such a fog of greyness and sadness stretching endlessly over the whole area. Everyone put their hearts and souls into trying to make it a special day, allowing the children to just be children again, as so many had, and I guess still do, have traumatic memories.

At the Listening Point we were providing refreshments, hot dogs (there lies a funny story) and ice creams. There were all the usual stalls and games, as well as donkey rides. The weather was pretty kind to us (apart from a couple of gusts of wind when people had to chase around retrieving their goods and leaflets). There was quite a good attendance and people made an effort to put on a display of a normal fun day, although things were far from normal.

Someone had dressed as a Disney character and was enticing the children to have photos taken with him. It was very obvious that none of the kids felt comfortable doing this and wanted to stay close with their families. A storyteller sat on the grass in front of our building weaving her magic to the eager ears of little people sitting in a circle around her, closely watched over by a family member. No one was willing to let their children have the freedom previously taken for granted in this safe and trusted community.

I remember Maria and myself entering into the tug of war competition. We didn't, as I recall, add much muscle to the proceedings, and got beaten twice (we really must get in some more practice!!!). Together with the fact I have never been able to stomach a frankfurter since!!!

We talk about the Fun Day, how it illustrates again the determination to make things as "normal as possible" for the children, and the moments of jarring when the awful events of the past few months were brought into mind and people felt guilty about "having fun".

Collective voice:
There was also almost a hint of hysteria in the air;
"We are going to have fun!!"

We've got to have a fun side too!
We can't afford to be in black and mourning forever.
We had a few who were coming into the centre.
And we needed the tissues... then they were out again having fun.

Then there was Maria, and the hotdogs, and the tea urn.
The hotdogs bubbling away in the urn!
That was hysterical really!
500 hot dog sausages,
50 sausages in each tin.

The organisers gave us a camping stove and a small saucepan,
and we couldn't heat them up properly.
Then, there was plan B!

Not sure whose idea it was
but –
We looked at the two tea urns,
We looked at each other,
and then we tipped them in!
The sausages bubbling in one of the urns.

Don't drink tea for some time!!

Towards the end of the day there was Maria.
She was on the tea urn getting flustered;
the urns stood side-by-side
(as that was where the plug socket was)
and she made someone coffee with the sausage-urn water!
Fortunately she remembered before he drank it!

And we laughed so much.
It was so good to laugh.

For months afterwards people using that urn probably thought their tea tasted strange!!

It's a good job I did not have any.
I am very allergic to hot dogs

(much laughter).

The person who loved the hot dogs was the new community policeman.
It was his first week I think.
He kept coming back and having more,
I think perhaps he felt safe with us.
I remember having a bubble thought go through my mind:
"If he gets food poisoning we will be in big trouble!"

It felt really important to remember that
'It is ok and important to have fun.'

Anne Marie comments:
I was not involved with the project then,
but I had been asked to film the event.
So I was filming.
But when I was confronted with that film,
I kept thinking, "What will other people think?"
Us, laughing and being happy when all this has been happening,
is happening.

That is other people's "should" and "oughts".
Their expectations,
and it is those that hold us from being free to feel
cultural expectations even?

As I watched that film back I was wondering,
'Would other people think this was disrespectful to laugh and have a nice time?"
But there was something about that re-engaging with laughter.
That was really important.
But even at the Fun Day you would suddenly see people freeze.
It was like as if a wave hit them.

Collective voice:
The policeman dressed up in this outfit;
you know,
enormous, furry suit.

They thought it would be quite fun for the children,
and he was the new recruit.
None of the children would have their photo taken with him though.
In the end Auntie Maria had to go with them,
a bit like the Pied Piper.

When they were coming into the storytelling tent,
they always brought an adult.

The ice cream van was there too,
and normally the kids would flock up,
but not this time, only with their parents.
It was painful to watch.

That kind of anxiety did not last terribly long, though, did it?
Soon the kids were back to having freedom again,
at least the ones I meet with
were roaming around the estate again
by the end of the summer.
But something of the innocence has been lost,
a concerted effort needed now for normalcy.

It seemed really important for the community, especially the children, that some kind of "normality" and "routine" was re-introduced. The early days following April's abduction were chaotic and filled with fear as searching became widespread and the media arrived.

The effects of trauma are often most acute where a person's existing world and safety (both physical and mental) are threatened (van der Kolk, Mc Farlane, and Weisaeth 1996). The first event to happen, the lantern parade, was known and loved – a familiar recurring festival. From a narrative therapy perspective, holding community events and celebrations could be thought of as an attempt to re-member or re-author the stories we live by (White 2007); engaging again with familiar people and positive events. Yet it seemed, even as we tried to re-engage with the familiar, it was still important to acknowledge the grief and loss. As previously noted, even for those not touched personally by the tragedy, often there were losses of hopes and dreams about what it meant to live in this community. Some recurring comments were:

"I always thought this was a safe place;" "I thought my children growing up here were safe;" "This place will never be the same now;" "The Lantern Procession will never be the same now."

Considerations and conclusions

- If the service set up in the wake of a tragedy is to be of assistance to the whole community then it needs to look beyond the remit of the project and support the community's own endeavours to re-connect with "normal" events and community happenings, and encourage community leaders.

- The grief process for those in the wider community affected by traumatic events will not necessarily follow the same pattern as that of the intimate family or families affected, and within the wider community each individual's experience and needs will differ.

- Grieving and recovery from trauma does not follow a consistent pattern. People in Machynlleth reported that there were times when they engaged with events as they always had (and enjoyed them) and other times when they were triggered in a number of different ways into remembering and feeling a range of emotions, including sadness, anger, fear and anxiety.

- Liaison with the police investigation and the police family liaison team ensures that planned community events can both be supported by, and sensitive to, the police, and any on-going investigation. The police press office can also manage media interest. Events in the first 12 months following April's abduction always brought intense media presence from across the world.

Chapter Ten

April's Garden

Sue's journal: May 2013
Sitting on April's bench, I eat a sandwich in the sun whilst I wait for Listening Point to open. The garden is becoming extremely pink. The trial is bringing horrific revelation after horrific revelation and as it does so more and more pink lights, toys and ribbons arrive and hang from the trees. A small pink dolls' house, teddies, a stork or some kind of bird, butterflies, flowers, a multitude of lights. I sense April here, though; I feel the love, the pain, the care that was the intention behind these gifts. I know some see only the pain, the rather over-bright pinkness, the horror of it all, and want to banish it from sight. But for me, I have to touch the realness of that pain, that loss. I have to sit here with my feet rooted into the ground where there is a connection with the little girl. How much of that reality I can bear I don't know; I am not sure I would want it every day, every hour of the day and night. I understand the pain it causes to others, but there is something real here, despite the frothy plastic pinkness; something real about the pain here, the love that flows from each fluttering pink thing which has been placed with care on and in the bare earth. I am reminded of "ashes to ashes" and my own and my family's mortality.

Community update April 2013

30th April 2013
"Trial starts in Mold of Mark Bridger accused of abducting and murdering schoolgirl April Jones from outside her home in Machynlleth in October 2012.

"The jury heard Mr Bridger undertook an "extensive clean-up operation" at his home, which included the disposal of April's body and her clothes.

"However, some evidence remained. Blood found in the living room, hallway and bathroom matched April's DNA, the jury was told.

"Ms Evans told the court bone fragments were found, and said the view of experts was bone fragments found in fire ashes at Mr Bridger's home were consistent with bone fragments from a juvenile human skull.

"Police found child pornography and photos of raped and murdered children including Holly Wells and Jessica Chapman, the Soham murder victims, on Mr Bridger's laptop computer, the jury was told."

South Wales Evening Post
http://www.southwales-eveningpost.co.uk/April-Jones-trial-child-porn-Mark-Bridger-s/story-18847003-detail/story.html#ixzz3YswMgPQ2

April's Garden

April's Garden, as it became known, was on the green between the houses on the Bryn-y-Gog estate. It started with a small flowering tree and a flowerbed.

Lisa remembers:

A bench was erected on the green as an everlasting memory, I believe was it was made by someone serving a jail sentence.

A working party of local residents set about marking out several areas to create a special garden in memory of the little girl who never came home. I remember we took out trays of tea and biscuits as they toiled with the digging, edging and planting.

We managed to help in some small way by getting a local building firm to donate some gravel to put on the beds in between the plants to stop the weeds.

It was beginning to take shape; very soon bulbs and flowers bursting forth looking fresh and beautiful. People from all around began bringing small items to place on the gardens – ornaments, angels and things that illuminated at night. Paul and Coral added to the collection with dolls and all manner of pink items that they had been sent. This continued with the arrival of a large dolls' house and pink wool wrapped around the trunk of a tree.

When the trial started there was increased activity in the garden. One of the gardeners told Lisa that they "thought it would be a lovely idea to try to get it looking beautiful for April's parents when they returned from the harrowing days at Mold court".

Many people from outside the area also wanted to visit the garden. We discuss this at one of our research meetings:

Collective voice:
A family came
(rather like the von Trapp family).
A woman with lots of beautifully dressed children.
They brought a bouquet of flowers for April's mother,
but she wasn't in.

Seven daughters;
they had come on the bus,
borrowed the money from her father and come to see the garden and April's parents were not in.
It was the mother's 40th birthday,

We invited them into the drop-in
and gave them cakes and juice;
I seem to remember that there were a lot of people in Listening Point that day.
Waves of people...
It was a bit spontaneous sometimes.
You were never sure what would happen,
but we were very game.

"We need some gravel for the garden?
We will give it a go.
How many sacks do you want?"

It is the funny things that happened too.
The lady with the bluebells in a bucket.
Do you remember her?
She did not want to go over to the garden
so she brought them to us instead.

These odd things used to happen.
The little boy who got his arm stuck in the letterbox!

He was playing outside with his toy cars, happily,
on the window ledge and shooting his cars through the letter box
in the wall.

The car got stuck, so he put his arm through the letterbox
from the outside.
He had a coat on, so got stuck and started to panic.
We got him out though!
But I panicked and thought
Oh my God, we may have to get the fire brigade.

Afterwards every time children passed the letterbox I felt like –
Oh no, not again.

Other visitors to the garden were not so welcome. The pink of the garden made a splendid backdrop for the national and international media, who used it regularly to update on progress in the investigation and the trial.

For some people, however, the garden was a painful reminder of the dreadful things that had happened to April. Lisa remembers:

> At night it was aglow with pink stars and bright lights. Some people living within sight of the garden reported that they had even considered moving because they found it too upsetting.

There seems to be a tradition now when someone has died suddenly traumatically of leaving flowers and tributes at, or near to, where they died or lived. Flowers left at the side of the road mark places where people were killed in accidents.

In a chapter on sacred sites set apart for remembrance, Elliott says of roadside tributes that

> … there is a link here, whether articulated in any real sense or not, to the blood spilt on the earth. This physical place is important as it connects the family to the violence which removed the life of the person (Elliott 2014, 144).

I wonder whether this garden somehow connects us with April; for some, is it part of the grieving or bereavement process?

Bereavement

Most theories of how we grieve and bereavement processes describe various phases of grief, including feelings of shock, disbelief, pain, and anger, and ultimately an acceptance and letting go of the person.

However Klass, Silverman and Nickman (1996) found in their research with a self-help group for bereaved parents that it was not so much a "letting go" that helped the parents move on but the intense interaction and a changing relationship with their dead children that helped them resolve their grief. One parent wrote:

> Will you forgive me if I go on?
> If you can't make this earthly journey through time with me,
> Will you then come along in my heart and wish me well?
> (Klass, Silverman and Nickman 1996, xvii).

The authors then go on to explore further how the challenge of bereavement is not so much to accept and "let go", but to accept a new and different relationship with the person they have lost – a re-membering of that relationship.

Within narrative therapy, re-membering[4] conversations are often used to connect with new ways of relating to the person who was lost. Maryam Burquan writes of her work with a bereaved woman:

> I was interested in asking questions according to the re-membering conversations map,[4] to gather richer descriptions about the contributions that the husband had made to her life, and the contributions that she had made to his life. I wanted to hear about a two-way account of this relationship as I thought this would assist to sustain her during these difficult times (Burquan 2006).

She goes on to describe how this honouring of this two-way relationship was significant to her client and that, although she accepted that her husband was dead, and in another world now, this

---

[4] For more information about Michael White's re-membering conversations map see www.dulwichcentre.com.au

acknowledgement of an on-going but different relationship was important to her.

Holding a conflicted space

Whatever our own feelings, within the project we had to hold the space for both those who found solace in the garden and those who found it extremely painful.

I speak with Ceri and Anne-Marie. It is difficult, I find, to write coherently about the garden: why it was important and why it was such a difficult place for some.

Ceri: I remember seeing an incredibly beautiful glass heart ornament
on a bush.
It was so beautiful.
There was so much love in it.

Anne Marie: Lots of people found it
incredibly painful to look at it though.

Ceri: People sometimes feel they haven't any right to be affected
in good or bad ways;
but where it touches personal things,
it affects people deeply.

Something I did after my son died.
People gave me lots of things,
little presents.
Things that were really "bizarre" as far as I was concerned.

They had for some reason thought this was precious,
and felt I should have it.
But they weren't things that I necessarily wanted.

But what I decided to do about all of those things
was to take the support and
the love from those things,
then I smashed them all up and

I buried them in the lane at the back of the garden.

I dug a big hole,
tore up the cards
and buried everything.

The flowers people had sent me.
I put the dead flowers in there.

I wanted to keep,
to squeeze, every drop of juice out of those gifts.
Everything that people intended for me;
the intention behind the gift
but I didn't want to make it into a memorial.

I didn't want to have a room in the house with
all those things in.
I knew that if you don't get rid of things
then they start to hold a heavy charge.
They start to have a presence of their own.

My experience of April's Garden
was that I understood.
I recognised the bush with that beautiful glass on it
as a sacred space.

And the garden.
People wanted to give things
and do things
but at some point it became a bit
heavily charged.

So that the things became more meaningful
than the giving of them.

People then were sensitive to the pain of those things,
not to the intention with which they were given.

They then started to really "not like it"

because of the pain of that.

In my personal life I deal with it by letting things change...
Because they do.
They don't stay static.

Sue: The things in the garden needed to change and move.

Ceri: The thing that happened in this community is still here
And it's about allowing it to change and move.
We will not always feel the same about it
And that is not bad at all.

Anne Marie: The garden was also perhaps
the need to have some tangible thing.
There was no body.
No funeral... at that point.
The garden perhaps was a tangible thing.
For a connection with April.

CHAPTER ELEVEN

THE TRIAL

This chapter is one that I seem to find hard to write. I find a multitude of other things to write and think about instead. It is perhaps, as Ò Tuama says, "the unwritable chapter" (Ò Tuama 2012). I find I can remember very little of that time. It is as if the four weeks of the trial never happened, although my journal records the moment when I heard the news about the verdict.

Sue's journal: May 2013
I laid awake again last night. The jury is still out. There is tangible tension here in Machynlleth. It feels oppressive; as if I cannot breathe. It is as if the whole community is holding its breath. What will happen in this place if they find him not guilty? I skirt around the thought. I cannot even think how we would go about finding a way of supporting the community if that happened. I am not really sure I know how we are going to support the community if he is found guilty. My fear is that the most difficult time is yet to come, as we turn from being "united in a quest for justice" to trying to get back to normal living, whatever that means.

I cannot bear the wait, or being here, so go with my husband into neighbouring Dolgellau. We are half way, on the road through the mountains, when I get the phone call. One of the family liaison officers, his voice choked with emotion, says just one word. Guilty… he can say no more. In that moment I find myself weeping with him, tears streaming down my face. Sentencing is to be later in the day. In that moment I feel relief; later comes the realisation that a "whole life sentence" is also what April's family, and indeed to a lesser extent all of us, face. We cannot undo what was done in that night of 1st October 2012, or what we know. There will never be "closure" or even justice, as one little girl will never grow up to adulthood.

I share this with the research group.

Sue: I am finding it really difficult to write about the trial, or even think about it.

Lisa: I was on holiday, I remember checking the internet and my husband saying, "You don't have to do that, you are on holiday." But I had to know. I just had to know.

Hope: I completely dissociated.
It was completely gone from my mind.
I put it straight out of my mind.
The trial.
I can't remember any of that.

Sue: We <u>were</u> there.
We opened Listening Point every week.
We were there.

Hope: It is all coming back to me now.
But I find it difficult to stay with it.

Trauma and dissociation

In our meetings we often talked about feeling "dissociated" or "dissociation", especially in relation to the days initially following April's disappearance and the four weeks of the trial. As Spiegel points out, trauma can be perceived as a "threat that may undermine many assumptions by which people live" (Spiegel 1991, 261). For all of us living in Machynlleth, the evidence coming from the trial was so shocking that many people were visibly traumatised, including us. To enable us to cope with the professional demands of the project, many of us dissociated; even now, some two years later, we find it difficult to piece together a coherent account of what happened.

Spiegel goes on to say:

> Dissociative defences, which allow individuals to compartmentalize perceptions and memories, seem to perform a dual function. They help victims separate themselves from the full impact of physical trauma while it is occurring, and, but in the same token, they may delay the necessary

working through and putting into perspective of these traumatic experiences after they have occurred (ibid, 261).

My diary entry made before my meeting with the research group to discuss the trial is interesting in that I described talking about the trial as "life threatening", even though I knew logically this was not so.

Sue's journal: March 2014
I am not sure what is going on. Perhaps I ought to stop writing? For some reason I feel paralysed with fear... Of what I do not know.

I have a meeting booked with the co-researchers as I find myself unable to write anything about the trial or April's Garden. Even the thought of talking about it seems somehow like a life-threatening event. My heart rate goes up, I want to avoid it. I don't understand. We did meet though, during the trial; we met each week as normal. I don't remember it being particularly different, nothing too terrible happened, but I am experiencing the remembering of it as if something traumatic happened.

Gradually, when we are all together, we do start to remember some of the facts from that time.

Ceri: I think that there was a lot of feeling going on in the town
When the trial was going on.

It stirred up a lot of anger.
It was very quiet the first day.
Sort of shocked quiet.

Sue: The first day was the one they had all those revelations about the forensic evidence.

Lisa: I remember you said there was going to be some pretty horrific things coming out.

Sue: We opened up and held
an impromptu drop-in session at Listening Point.
We didn't feel it was right, not to be open,
with all that was going on.

Some of us knew what was going to come out,
but a lot of those in the community didn't.
And in the lead up to the trial there was a lot of tension.
People wanting to know what happened,
And yet dreading to know what happened.

Hope: Something I've remembered –
Something that struck me, was that
April's parents were going up to the trial
and I remember putting myself in that position
and thinking
I am not sure that I could have done that.
They faced him every day.

Lisa: That must have taken amazing inner strength.
I could not manage it.

Sue: We lived through the trial back in Mach.
But I don't remember us being particularly different or upset
(perhaps I am still dissociated)
It still felt light.
People dropped in more
But they didn't want to talk about it.
We were not gloomy.

Hope: No. Well I was completely dissociated from it –
Just carrying on.

We discuss whether dissociation was helpful to us in continuing to function. Spiegel considers that "a predominant defence against trauma is a sense of 'psychological detachment' from the physical environment" (Spiegel 1991, 263). Lisa points out:

For each and everyone of us there were certain points when we had to stand back a bit.
I don't think you are consciously aware of doing it,
But perhaps it is a natural sort of protection.

Hope: I was certainly protecting myself
so that I could be there for those who came in.

Sue: I can remember now as we speak,
people coming in and out of the centre.
And they were either angry or –

They were upset or they were leaving gifts at the garden.
So many gifts in that time.
It got pinker and more extreme.

Ceri: Others just came in and had tea and kept everything inside them.
People were very shocked at some of the details
But still not talking about it.
Never discussing it.
Sometimes dissociation is our friend,
it protects us from being overwhelmed.
We naturally do that.

Sue: Even if we don't call it that.

Ceri: When something is too bad
We don't take it all in at first
We have to absorb it slowly.

Sue: Perhaps we are still in the process of that.

Ceri: I can remember thinking a lot about the police at the time.
How did they manage?
How did they manage to go round and be ordinary with people knowing what they knew?
While they were having their own reactions?

Anne Marie: The journalists,
one I know was there every day.
The impact of that.

There are many approaches to working with trauma. As a therapist, my preferred way of working is to use a narrative approach that seeks to avoid the re-telling of events in ways that re-traumatise people but enables them to find ways of converting the fragmented traumatic memories, laden with affect, into more historic accounts of something that has happened in the past within a particular time frame. The aim is to re-author the event (White 2006) as something painful that happened in the past rather than re-experience the original pain in the here and now.

White makes the point that:

> Because dissociated memories stand outside of and are independent of people's lives, they are timeless memories; these memories are apart from the storylines of people's lives, which are constituted of experiences linked in sequences across time according to specific themes. Being located on the outside of the dimension of time, these traumatic memories have no beginning and no end. When traumatic memories are beyond time in this way, there is always the potential for particular circumstances to trigger the re-living of the memories in real time. These traumatic memories are re-lived as present experience and the outcome is re-traumatisation (White 2006, 78).

I was very conscious that, in speaking about our memories of the trial, we ran the risk of triggering memories that would lead to re-traumatisation. I wanted to ensure that this did not happen.

White goes on to say that:

> In order to re-associate dissociated memories, it is necessary to restore these half memories to full memories. In other words, the task is to resurrect that which is erased in dissociated memory – that is, people's responses to what they were being put through, and the foundations of these responses. This resurrection is restorative of a sense of personal agency, one that is in harmony with the person's "preferred sense of self". This is the "sense of myself" that provides an experience of continuity of personhood through the many episodes of one's history (White 2006, 79).

When we met to talk about the trial I was keen to engage in conversations that linked any fragmented traumatic memories with what we did within Listening Point, the purpose and intentions of our actions, and place this within a coherent history of the town and other, personal events, and to render the dissociation "normal in the circumstance we found ourselves".

The dissociation we experienced was, in my view, a very valid way of coping with the shocking facts that were emerging that threatened to damage our beliefs about Machynlleth as a "safe place" and our moral beliefs about caring for children, the sanctity of life, and our many other personal values and beliefs. We were often unable to process the thoughts and feelings we had at the time because we had to provide the "professional space" for others. Returning to our values and beliefs and seeing them as the reason why we responded was helpful in enabling us to begin to re-associate these memories.

We used the remainder of that research meeting as a "private therapeutic space" in which to explore further our thoughts and feelings around the trial and what Hope described as "the elephant in the room" – Mark Bridger.

We allowed ourselves to feel, to consider, where we were, wherever that was for each of us. It felt healthy, even if it was painful, to have that discussion, although, as author, I do not feel it is right to share the details here. For me what subsequently changed was that the fear dissipated, to be replaced by a more linear memory of events that took place over a specific time period.

We also spoke about forgiveness, and how this was such a difficult and emotive subject. I recalled a community leader stating in an interview soon after April had been abducted that "the community would perhaps in time learn to forgive", and that the reaction from many was extremely hostile. The interviewer asking the unprepared question, "will the community forgive Mark Bridger" felt to me abusive; I complained to the BBC programme makers.

I am not sure I am ready to grapple with forgiveness yet, or if I will ever be; I am still trying to assess and take on the enormity of the pain suffered by April's parents, her family, the police teams, the wider community and others. Until I allow myself to consider this, I cannot know what it is that I am forgiving, or how I might do that, or even what I mean by forgiveness. I accept this is a limitation, but also feel that it is perhaps a tribute to how much I value children and their care.

These are some of our thoughts about forgiveness that we felt it would be helpful to share.

Collective:
Perhaps forgiveness is about
forgiveness of a person
not an action.

If the action is totally unacceptable,
it will always be totally unacceptable.
Always.

Perhaps it is about letting go of the anger,
getting rid of the baggage.
You are the one that has to carry that baggage,
not the other person.

But sometimes
you need a big lot of oil.
Or can't.
And letting go is so hard.

Because letting go can feel like –
Disloyalty.
Disloyalty to April.

These were really difficult conversations,
things we cannot say anywhere else.
It is good to get it out really.

We are not really agreeing with each other.
Or trying to.
But it makes us think about these things.

There is so much that cannot be said here in this town at the moment.
This is perhaps the only place we can talk.

If we don't ever speak about it
it gets stuck.
It festers.
We will never know what we feel.

There is a need to blame someone –
The media,
Mark Bridger.

I recognise that this chapter may seem incomplete. I apologise for that. Perhaps, however, this is because we are only just at the beginning of a process of personal reflection that may take time. I hope that what we have written relays something of the complexity of working with, and writing about, matters that so intimately affected us as co-researchers and writers. Hopefully, each word painfully written will have given some insight into the experience of living through a child murder trial from our particular perspectives as community members.

Through the four weeks of the trial, Machynlleth was again at the centre of international media scrutiny. Each time the Listening Point opened its doors we had to make our way into the centre through the gathered TV cameras and reporters who parked in our car park. Our most amusing fundraising effort was when Maria charged reporters £5 to use our toilet facilities!

Visitors poured in from all over the world, leaving tributes in April's Garden and visiting the project. Local people retreated as each day brought more shocking revelations from the court. Each day someone would visit the centre and say "When will this all be over?"

Considerations and conclusions

- Project workers are not immune to being traumatised by the stories others tell them, or by the events going on around them. It is important to address this in support sessions for volunteers and workers, both at the time, but also following the end of the project.

- There are many ways of working with trauma, but within a narrative approach there needs to be, as White points out, "priority given to the redevelopment and reinvigoration of a 'sense of myself' in work with people who have been subject to trauma" and that "revitalisation is essential in establishing a context for re-association of dissociated memory" (White 2006, 81).

- When supporting a project that involves a protracted police investigation and trial, it is not always possible for the police to warn anyone about the shocking nature of the evidence (otherwise the perpetrator could claim they were not being given a fair trial). It is difficult, however, for those who do know what will be coming out in the evidence as they are unable to talk about their thoughts and feelings, which can lead to a sense of isolation.

CHAPTER TWELVE

WORKING WITH YOUNG PEOPLE

Sue's journal: July 2013
The schools are just about to break up for the summer holidays. As I look out from the centre at the mass of pink that has become "April's Garden" I am afraid for the children on the estate. School in some ways has been a real blessing, holding the children safe within very secure boundaries. For a few hours a day the children are held in routines of regular lessons and routines. Here, on the estate, the earth seems to tremble with emotion; parents struggle as they try to comprehend the enormity of what has happened to another family, their neighbours; the pinkness an attempt to blot out the ugliness and pain.

What will happen when the routine of school finishes? I know that at Listening Point we do not have the resources, expertise or woman power to do other than provide a safe haven. I hope that there are others who can step in.

Community update August 2013

5th August 2013
"An Eddie Stobart lorry has been named in honour of five-year-old April Jones in her home town.

"The haulage company, which gives all its cabs female names, named its latest in memory of the girl who was abducted and murdered in Machynlleth, Powys. The idea came from a Shropshire couple who joined the search for April." www.bbc.co.uk/news

8th August 2013
"I came from London to see the 'hugging tree' and April's Garden. I needed to say a prayer for her here." (Letter left in drop-in centre)

Therapeutic support for young people and families

Young people and families were very much in my thoughts when we started Listening Point. I remained aware that, as a drop-in and counselling service, we were not really equipped to deal with the specific needs of young people; especially those who were at school with, and lived alongside, April.

Some families and children attended the drop-in sessions, and we held a number of creative therapeutic art sessions, facilitated by an art psychotherapist (see Chapter 13). We also referred some young people to independent practitioners who had experience and training in working with children and young people.

Back in the autumn of 2012, while I was gathering information in preparation for the project, I was aware that Cruse Powys was working in both the schools in Machynlleth. I went to see them to understand more about what they were doing, and to ask if they would provide some initial training for Listening Point volunteers.

This is Cruse's comment on their work with families and children in Machynlleth:

> At the beginning of October 2012, when April was first reported as missing, we received an urgent call for help to provide support for the school communities in Machynlleth. The call was made by Dr Alun Flynn, the Chief Educational Psychologist from Powys County Council, who knows of our work in supporting adults, children and young people.
>
> We responded by organising a small team of our volunteers to provide a presence and offer support and training to both school communities. The support was in the form of one-to-one and group support to parents, teachers, classroom assistants, other school staff and children. We also gave some training to teachers and classroom assistants on how to support the children. We felt very privileged to be welcomed into the communities during this stressful situation and to offer some help. We have continued to keep a small team of volunteers available for as and when they are needed, and we have received messages of appreciation for our

support from both schools. As a result of a request from Sue Dale, from the CCSW, we provided some training for the recently recruited volunteers for the drop-in centre in Machynlleth.

Our charity continues to offer a free service, which is given by skilled volunteers and, as a result, Cruse in Powys relies heavily on donations to cover the cost of keeping our service in Powys running.

Hope, who worked with children and young people in a number of settings within Listening Point and beyond, reflects on her experiences:

I remember working with children and young people at the Listening Point and finding them wonderful and honest, sharing what their parents were saying in an unconscious, matter of fact way. Like "my mum says..." and "my uncle thinks..." – the vulnerability, the openness, the trusting in sharp juxtaposition to the predator Mark Bridger.

A part of me wanting to scoop them up and keep them safe and then the counsellor part wilfully keeping that safe space open for all of their expression. I think at these times I felt the pain most deeply.

What gives me solace is seeing those same young people moving on, growing up, being bright, active members of the community. I see them in the town carnival, in the local shops doing errands, breaking through the fear and just living, really. They won't forget, I won't forget, but he will not be our keeper, he won't be given that power.

Ffilm Club

I first met Anne Marie some months after Listening Point had moved to the Bryn-y-Gog estate. She approached me about a film project; she had been undertaking an ethnographic community research project in Machynlleth, using the medium of film. This involved interacting with the local community and filming the carnivals and many other community events over a period of some time. The Ffilm Club started some months after April was abducted and was instigated by a group of young people who wanted to make and edit their own films about their experiences. Anne Marie approached me, in my role as narrative researcher and counselling supervisor, as she had observed that the young people were using the medium of film-making as a "therapeutic tool" and she felt that she did not have the experience or therapeutic training to support them. I agreed to supervise the therapeutic element of the project, and an experienced counsellor from Listening Point agreed to work with her to provide group and, where needed, individual therapeutic support to the young people. I was concerned that the process of making films together should not harm the young people in any way. My journal from that time notes my relief at finding someone who was able to engage with young people in a way that was meaningful to them:

> *Sue's journal: September 2013*
> *I feel really excited, and feel a mixture of "this is really good" and "this is really scary". Good, because I can see the potential for therapeutic benefit for a group of traumatised young people, and the skill and care with which Anne Marie works, and scary because it is outside the norms of "counselling", and it is important that the young people are safe and not damaged by this process. If we can encompass it within the "narrative therapy" frame then I think it will have a structure that can prove very fruitful.*
>
> *I have also suggested that Hope and/or Sue W (who are counsellors experienced in working both with groups and with young people) may be people who would offer support such that they can hold the "therapeutic content", and Anne Marie can concentrate on holding the filming and editing and co-researching bit.*
>
> *Note to self: Try to get Level 1 Narrative Therapy training for both Anne Marie and other Listening Point volunteers.*

Conversations about methodology, research **and the Ffilm project**

Anne Marie:

I trained as a documentary filmmaker and spent some 15 years working in the television industry. My films had mostly been about what used to be called "social issue", but I found it increasingly difficult to accept the requirements of broadcast television – the pressure to encourage conflict between protagonists in order to create "drama", and the requirement to get "informants" to sign consent forms *before* filming, thus signing away their rights to any control over the way material was used. As a reaction to what I considered to be "exploitation", I considered it more ethical to gain consent as the film evolved, thus enabling participants to make more participatory and informed choices.

Before moving to Machynlleth in 1995 I had been involved in participatory video[5] work projects around the UK. After moving to Machynlleth in 1995 I became interested in using video as a tool to encourage Welsh rural communities to express and act collectively on their feelings and experiences about local issues in what Downing and colleagues describe as "capacity building" (Downing, Rosenthall and Hudson 2002). I set up and ran a community video organisation with my colleague Ioana Sawtell. This interest then led me to complete an MPhil in Ethnographic Documentary, which gave an opportunity to work with the communities around Machynlleth and to further develop these collaborative and reflexive film-making techniques, without the usual time constraints of voluntary sector funding. This work formed the basis of the children's video project discussed in this chapter.

During the search for April, like most local people I wanted to be in some way useful and active. I had (somewhat unexpectedly) become involved with the teams providing food for the police and search teams and wanted to document, explore and celebrate the powerful process of the community working so closely together.

However, it felt very inappropriate for me to pick up the camera at all as so many people were very upset and distrustful of the media. As I helped alongside others, local residents seemed to forget my professional identity as a filmmaker and, on the one occasion I did try to do some filming, local people I knew were shocked and horrified, asking if I "worked for the media". It has been interesting to note how film-making colleagues who did not live in the area

---

[5] See Jackie Shaw and Clive Robertson's book *Participatory Video: A Practical Approach to Using Video Creatively in Group Development Work* (Shaw and Robertson 1997) for more information.

asked whether I was filming what was happening at the time, and subsequent events to do with the case. It seemed impossible to explain to them how insensitive and inappropriate this would feel, and why I had no desire to do this.

This was my only attempt at filming for some months, until many months later I felt "driven" to document the pink ribbons tied to every available post, gate and tree for miles around (and indeed, across Wales and the UK), by which time being out and about with a camera seemed to be less traumatic for people locally, and in fact many showed a positive interest in what I was doing. It was during this time that two boys who lived on the estate first approached me and asked if they could work with me to "tell stories" on video.

After careful thought and discussion with the young people's parents, I agreed. I had just been offered a place to do a practice-based PhD to further explore the community engagement work I had been doing locally with adults, but I felt that this direct request from the young people was more urgent. More local children and young people became involved and thus began a (more than) two-year journey with them. This was undertaken on a voluntary basis with the full support and involvement of the young people's families and with crucial supervision support from Dr Susan Dale, a psychotherapist and supervisor running the Listening Point project, and from Hugh Fox from the Institute of Narrative Therapy (see further below).

I also recognise that I had a strong personal need to try to process and make some sense out of what had happened to us in Machynlleth. Like most documentary film-makers I am accustomed to using the film-making journey as a means of exploring thorny ideas and questions with people who have more direct experience of the issue in question. As a local resident and insider ethnographer (Naaeke et al. 2010), it did not feel possible to embark upon such a journey with the local (adult) community because of their negative experiences and associations with the media. However, the young people were very anxious to be involved, and saw it as a positive opportunity.

Certainly, when I started this project my main motivation was to provide an enjoyable activity for local children who had been so strongly affected by April's death, and I felt that the priority was to create a safe, consistent and non-judgemental space. I knew from my own professional experience that video could be a very effective means of achieving this, but it is worth bearing in mind that video may be just one tool, and other skills and techniques could perhaps be used – the key is in bringing the right social and group development skills to the process. As well as being fun for children to use, set up in a sensitive and trusting way, the camera encourages a certain gravitas and can be used to introduce a time and space for focused reflection and thought, which can be fruitfully returned to again and again.

I felt a need to use the skills I had accumulated over many years' experience in the service of the community and had been looking for a way to do this. I had previously worked with video with the head of the local primary school, but with the trial coming up it did not feel appropriate for the school to formally support a new initiative. As a result, when I was unexpectedly asked to do this work by local children, I was more than happy to do so. I knew from previous experience of working with communities with respect to homelessness, domestic violence and self-harm, that these very difficult circumstances in Machynlleth would present a challenging project. I was clear that it would need to be set up very carefully, using extensive prior experience and support.

Despite having met with the young people's parents and gained their permission in February 2013, it took me six more months to feel ready to actually begin the process.

I was due to start doctoral studies the following September and, as community research was very much in my mind by this point, I explored whether this project could be used for this purpose. This provided a secondary motivation for the project and gave a clear research methodology for any publication of the footage. I explained this to the young people and their families and we developed a method of working that I hoped would meet both these objectives successfully without harm being done. This is, of course, very difficult to measure in any quantifiable sense (although detailed sessional logs and an "ethnographic diary" were kept), but I feel confident that there have been real benefits to the project for the young people taking part. As the children grow up they have been increasingly able to reflect and offer their evaluation on the process, and it will be interesting to continue this evaluation as part of a longitudinal study.

How Ffilm Club ran

I met with the young people once a week between July 2013 and November 2014. I then continued working with one of the original participants on an occasional one-to-one basis, with the others occasionally involved in editing as co-researchers (this is currently on-going). The name Ffilm Club was how the young people habitually referred to the group, and reflects the fact that some of the children were first language Welsh speakers and others spoke English as their first language (*ffilm* is the Welsh word for film).

For the first three months we met on the Bryn-y-Gog estate and filmed there, or around the town, depending on what the young people wanted to do. I would arrange a meeting at a central location and then together we wandered around looking for things to film, gathering other children on the way who wanted to take part (this again needed parental or caretaker permission before they could be involved). Before long a group of young people would usually be waiting for me to arrive on my bike with the video equipment, and they would rush over to help unload before deciding what we were going to do. It was during this period that I approached Sue to talk about supervision support, as I was aware that some of the filming and conversations with the young people were focused on April's murder.

With winter and long nights drawing in, we accepted an offer to use the Listening Point building on Bryn-y-Gog, and we used this as our base until October 2014, after which I continue to work with small groups or one-to-one at the edit room I rented locally.

Initially the filming outside was with a group of between three and ten children and young people, aged between f5 and 14 years. After moving to the Listening Point centre, I worked alongside a qualified counsellor with a closed group of between three and five young people aged 10–15 years for the remainder of the project. Having a second volunteer who was a counsellor meant that there was someone with therapeutic expertise available to undertake any one-to-one work that might be required for part of a session, or to support sessions. This alleviated some of the pressure I occasionally felt in maintaining a safe, boundaried space. In good weather we would use the Listening Point as a base from where we could go to film outside. In bad weather, or in the winter when it was already dark and the young people arrived after school, we used the camera to play indoor games; Chinese Whispers was especially popular. (See Shaw and Robertson (1997) for some suggestions for games using video.)

The supporting counsellor and I would meet at the centre; the young people would eat a snack (or would raid the kitchen for biscuits – it quickly became apparent that we needed to make sure they ate when they arrived at the session to fill the energy gap between school and tea). We then discussed how their previous week and the day had been and what they wanted to do in the session. I would then get them to set up the camera equipment, with varying degrees of success, depending on how co-operative they were feeling. Any challenging behaviour or issues were discussed and ground rules were drawn up by them, in discussion with us, and were often returned to in subsequent sessions. The young people would often claim to have no idea what they wanted to do in the session. Sometimes they took up our suggestions for filming, but more often they came up with some ideas of their own. They were keen on re-enacting television panel game shows and performing their favourite songs. Sometimes we went for bike rides or trips out to local attractions, which we all really enjoyed, and we incorporated filming into these trips.

As often as possible we watched back what they'd filmed in that session. It seemed very important that the young people saw themselves (and the workers) on screen as often as possible, so that they had an understanding of the process.

We worked with at least two cameras during the sessions, taking turns to film each other and filming both the "performances" to camera and the filming process. Control over filming lay largely with the young people, but I would often ask if I could document a discussion or activity on film as part of the research. They soon became very familiar with this, and began to decide for themselves if a conversation or query was worth documenting, and would take a camera accordingly. Sometimes they refused my requests, which was fine with me, as I tried to keep my own research agenda to a minimum and prioritise the fun and personal development aspect of the work. We also at times used art and craftwork and writing, both for fun and a means to explore issues and concerns. The young people usually initiated the craftwork or writing,, but as facilitators we would sometimes suggest this in order to work through a group or individual issue.

The sessions usually ran for two to three hours. It was recommended initially that I keep the sessions strictly boundaried to one hour, but we found that an hour was far too short to allow the participants to arrive, settle and focus on some work, so the length was expanded to fit around what we were doing. The young people also highly valued the "fun" aspect of the sessions and the deeper discussions about issues that arose from them and from their daily lives. Important issues often arose towards the end of the session, and could take some time to work through. Outside we filmed around the estate, or walked up the local hillside, "The Crag", or to visit the "hugging tree", and many interesting discussions took place in fields or on footpaths, walking or sitting, as the mood took us.

Sue W, one of the counsellors who supported Anne Marie at Ffilm Club, remembers:

During the months I worked with the young people we went to various locations around Machynlleth, filming, and went on walks and picnics and the occasional bike ride. During this time it became apparent how much the loss of April Jones had impacted on the children and the community they lived in. This was especially so when one evening we walked up to the "hugging tree" just outside of Machynlleth: it had been decorated so beautifully with an array of pink bows and ribbons. The young people shared their stories of where they were when April disappeared, and how it had changed their lives from that moment on. In particular, they commented on how they all used to leave school and congregate to play on the green together. However, afterwards it was so quiet and all the children and young people were kept indoors.

In setting up the Ffilm Club, it felt very important to give the young people a safe, comfortable place to come to each week and an opportunity to express themselves through film. One of the young people had a birthday whilst the club was running and a party was organised for her. I felt that this was a positive experience all round, as the children each contributed to the party and balloons were blown up, banners produced and a birthday cake made. It was a privilege to be part of the group and, much as the loss of April greatly affected the children and their community, I was also very moved that these same young people showed resilience and were able to work together to find ways to move forward in their lives.

Anne Marie goes on to describe how Ffilm Club worked:

I encouraged larger groups to make drama pieces that would give all of them a useful role, but with smaller groups we could go further afield and make short reportage pieces on local places such as the community garden. We also travelled around the local area on foot or by bicycle to do filming, and by car if the chosen locations were some miles away, and this travel added time to the sessions. We also filmed community events such as the letting off balloons for April's birthday, and the Fun Day.

However, a lack of strict time keeping did sometimes make it hard to end sessions and persuade the young people to go home, which could be tiring for us as facilitators, especially as we had little recourse to traditional authoritarian or parental discipline. However, I felt strongly that this all helped to create an especially positive atmosphere in which the young people could explore difficult issues, learn new skills and improve their communication and social skills whilst having fun.

November 2014 saw the ending of our charitable support and the closure of the Ffilm Club group in a formal sense. However, with the agreement of the families, I continued to work on an informal basis with one child co-researcher, and with input from other group members, as part of the research process.

How does narrative therapy fit with the film making?

When Anne Marie spoke to me about the Ffilm Club project, I was aware that she needed an ethical framework and some therapeutic input to ensure that her young participants remained "safe", and also that she needed a therapeutic framework that matched what she described as a "shared anthropology" [6] methodology that comes from a socially-constructed view of the world.

In respect of the ethical framework, we ensured that the work carried out in Ffilm Club met the commitments, values, principles and ethics of BACP's Ethical Framework (BACP, 2013, 2015). Mapping her post-structuralist position against therapeutic methodologies, the most obvious therapeutic model to suggest was narrative therapy, which as previously explained, also sees reality as socially constructed. From a narrative therapy perspective, young people meeting together and using film to tell their stories and edit and retell them would, I felt, enable them to "re-author" and "re-member" their stories within a safe setting. These stories currently included the shocking abduction and murder of one of the children they knew, by a man who was the father of other children who lived in their community, but they changed over time to wider descriptions of their lives and their hopes and dreams.

Offering more traditional counselling alongside the Ffilm Club project could be seen as controversial. This was because the person-centred

---

[6] For more information about "shared anthropology" see http://oxfordindex.oup.com/view/10.7208/chicago/9780226327167.003.0015

methodology (embraced by the counselling practitioners) comes from a Rogerian understanding that each person has within themselves "all that is needed to grow, become and actualise" (Rogers 1961; 1978). This description embraces an implicit statement that there is some intrinsic "reality" somewhere deep inside all of us. Counsellors often consider that a "real self" can be found if we peel back enough layers and look hard enough (Rowan 1983). A narrative therapist, conversely, would not consider looking for a "real self" but would look to change the "thin, problem-saturated stories" to "thicker richer descriptions of their life" (White and Epston 1990) to enable people to constantly reconstruct their sense of selves and identities. As previously explained, the methodology comes from a position of social constructionism: i.e. we make sense of our lives, and create reality through the relationships we create and the stories we tell about them.

For example, a hypothetical client, someone who has moved into the area with two young children, could perhaps comment:

> "April's Garden… It makes me feel… It makes me very angry!"

A person-centred practitioner's response to this might be to reflect this statement back to the client, but to change the nuance such that it becomes a question:

> "April's Garden. It makes you very angry?"

This could encourage the client to speak more about being "angry" and what this means. Or, they might say something like:

> "I notice you say that you feel angry about April's Garden, but as you say it there are tears in your eyes. I am wondering whether it is just 'angry' or whether there is something else?"

This could encourage the client to explore another feeling that may exist alongside "angry", or to speak about the anger in more depth. The "anger" is embedded into a felt sense. You "feel angry".

They are both the kind of questions that draw the person into an exploration of their inner world, into making sense of their thoughts feelings and behaviour so that they feel more "whole" or better able to integrate the feelings into their sense of being in the world.

A narrative therapist would, perhaps, take a different stance. They would listen attentively to the person but might respond with what White describes as "curious questions" (White 2007a), such as:

> "I notice that anger affects you when you think about the garden. I am wondering what kind of effect this has on your life?"

Here the "anger" is treated as the "problem", not the person. Anger is externalised, or seen as separate from the person, so that it can be explored in terms of other aspects of the person's life. Really good examples of externalising conversations in action can be found in Michael White's *Fear Busting and Monster Training* (White 1984; 1985), and my own example of *The Grilling of Mr B* (Dale 2009).

A narrative therapist may also be interested in exploring whether the anger relates to any hopes and values the person feels have been damaged or transgressed. They might ask, for example:

> "I am wondering what this 'anger' says about your hopes and dreams for living in this area."

Anger may then be seen as not necessarily negative but as a tribute or testimony to what has been lost. In the case of our hypothetical client, this could be hopes of a safe new life for their children in the country, or that paying respect to someone who has died should be a private act, or any number of values or hopes that that person holds.

White speaks of the narrative therapist's need to "scaffold" and move with the client:

> … mapping of the effects/influence of the problem through the various domains of living in which complications are identified (home, workplace, school, peer contexts; familial relationships, one's relationship with oneself, friendships; purposes, hopes, dreams, aspirations and values; life's horizons, one's future possibilities etc.(White 2005, 5)

Although the epistemological roots of the approaches were very different, the counsellors were both experienced practitioners who came from an integrative position; they were already using strands from other methodologies that fitted with Rogers' core conditions of "acceptance, unconditional positive regard and empathy" (Rogers 1961). The young people felt empathically listened to and that their views, needs and choices were respected; they experienced the core conditions set out within person-centred practice and were encouraged to explore what this event had meant to them in terms of their hopes and dreams, and to build a story that was thicker and richer than just that of April being murdered.

In practice, within the Ffilm Club the core conditions blended seamlessly with the re-authoring process of narrative therapy. It helped, I feel, that Anne Marie had a basic understanding of counselling theory, and that both counsellors involved in the project had basic training in narrative therapy (in addition to their core counselling training), so were able to find ways of integrating strands from each within a post-structuralist project. In one-to-one sessions the approach was more "person-centred"; within the group settings it was based more on "narrative therapy".

I was also keen to ensure that Anne Marie and the counsellors would be well supported and supervised in their work. My role was to offer consultative supervision to Anne Marie in respect of the overview, the interface between counselling, narrative therapy and research and practical aspects of the project. As Anne Marie notes above, she also contracted with an eminent narrative therapy supervisor to receive clinical supervision for the narrative therapy interventions with the young people. The counsellors both had independent clinical supervision and we provided all three with narrative therapy training in early 2014.

> Anne Marie: Sue had invited all those involved in the Listening Point to attend a week-long, Level 1 Narrative Therapy course in January 2014. I found this training invaluable. I was able to directly put some of it into practice with the young people at Ffilm Club, using it to direct the overall trajectory of this project, and apply it to other professional reflexive film projects that I subsequently undertook. Hugh Fox from the Institute of Narrative Therapy facilitated the training, as well as giving me monthly supervision sessions. Hugh's insights on the progress of the project through the lens of narrative therapy and his suggestions about using the technique as a way of dealing with the various issues arising in Ffilm Club were a valuable addition to my supervision with Sue. I felt quite inexperienced in using narrative therapy, but I think my tentative interventions were helpful, and it was a useful guide to keeping the overall trajectory of the project safe and positive.

Film-making and participatory video often involve the telling of stories and the development of coherent narratives. As narrative therapy approaches use re-narrativisation as a tool for personal recovery, it appealed to me as a useful additional tool in the participatory film-making process. I felt that this approach would be in harmony with my own aims of working with people locally to re-narrate the community's recovery, by bringing to the fore any positives that could be elicited from the trauma and maintaining important community values such as supporting the young people's independence and the continuation of regular community events and celebrations. It also proved to be a helpful guide for both the safe telling and reconfiguring of stories by both individuals and groups (see, for example, Sara Walther's work on housing estates in Manchester (Walther 2010)), and in ensuring that the overall direction of the project remained positive. Inviting others to be involved in the re-narrating is a key tenet of the process of validating the newly-formed preferred account; this outsider witnessing (White 2000) is a deliberate intervention that invites other trusted people to witness the person at the centre of the process tell their story, and then to express how hearing that story has allowed them to reflect on how they might approach issues in their own lives. Certainly using outsider witnessing techniques on film with the young people seemed to work well within the group, and we often discussed screening their work with an audience of invited guests, but the young people were not quite ready to take this step by the time the project came to an end.

Reflecting on these processes has enabled me to recognise the usefulness of this dual approach, which I consider reinforced the young people's sense of value and worth. I am aware that narrative therapy also has applications in family work, and I intend to explore this further as the research process unfolds, and I plan future publications.

Considerations and conclusions

Sue and Anne Marie:
Working therapeutically with children and young people, or within community settings as outlined within this chapter, is a very specialist activity. It is important that people with experience and relevant qualifications undertake the work, and that the work is supervised by skilled, experienced practitioners. Where families and young people accessed the general Listening Point services (through the drop-in, helpline, or creative therapeutic art days), they were usually supported by one or both of their parents, and supervised by either Sue Dale or by another counsellor with considerable experience of working with children and young people. Counselling referrals, where requested, were outsourced to practitioners with specific experience of working with children and young people..

Anne Marie will be independently publishing information about her research and detailed observations and suggestions for participatory video projects, but the following are considered the basic prerequisites for setting up any such project for young people.

- Workers need to have the necessary skills experience and training to do the work, including participatory video work. If therapy or counselling sessions are offered, this should be undertaken by counsellors or therapists who have a recognised professional qualification in working with children and young people.

- Professional independent supervision and line management (not necessarily from the same person) must be in place. It is worth noting that the BACP Ethical Framework for the Counselling Professions (BACP, 2015) points out that supervision is not just for counsellors and psychotherapists, but for

  > anyone providing therapeutically-based services, working in roles that require regularly giving or receiving emotionally challenging communications, or engaging in relationally complex and challenging roles' (BACP 2015, Good Practice point 61).

- Clear child protection policies and lines of referral must be agreed in case a safeguarding or child protection issue is identified. This will enable swift action to be taken should any serious issues or disclosures arise.

- Insurance cover (which CCSW provided for the Listening Point and the Ffilm club) should be in place to provide professional indemnity and professional public liability cover.

- The venue should be suitable and safe. It can be helpful to have a regular venue that the young people can have ownership of – one they feel they can use regularly and as they wish, within reason, and feel secure in.

- Therapeutic or community work with children and young people require facilitators and counsellors to have an up-to-date Disclosure and Barring Service (DBS) check. Again CCSW, as a registered charity, was able to arrange this for Ffilm Club and the Listening Point, but counsellors and other practitioners in private practice can also apply https://www.gov.uk/disclosure-barring-service-check/overview.

- It is important for young people to be aware of the boundaries of time, space and behaviour, and any limits to confidentiality of the material they are working with and sharing. Interpersonal boundaries are also important. For example, the levels of self-disclosure on the part of facilitators (young people are naturally curious), and relationships between members of the group need careful negotiation.

- It is important to agree basic ground rules for behaviour within sessions. In Ffilm Club the young people often added and rewrote the rules to meet different circumstances. Sometimes it was easier to film the ground rules as many of the children had dyslexia and found reading and writing challenging as a medium for communication.

Chapter Thirteen

Knitting, Creativity and Laughter

Sue's journal: October 2013
I was late arriving at the drop-in today; numerous phone calls and stress. Press wanting interviews; the same question again: "How do people feel about…?"

How can I possibly answer that? Frustration mingles with overwhelming sadness. We are here again and still there is no end. I think about last week and am lost in memories of April's funeral.

The church service was so hard in many different ways. The BBC was ensconced in the town and church from dawn, filming and directing our moves like the unfolding of a film script. People arriving in the church clad uncomfortably in pink; here in this Welsh town funerals are "always black". One man tells me he is afraid. My feeling is that our collective fear permeates the very stones of the church; communal gritted teeth barring the tears: "I cannot cry, this is not my tragedy," an elderly lady tells me. The words like a mantra echo in my head as I walk endlessly up and down the aisle, welcoming the terrified as they take their seats. This is another family's tragedy but it feels like my own; it feels like my child has died. There is a sense of standing firm (despite our own personal feelings) against the unfairness of the small, white, incredibly light coffin. My enmeshment in the community continues as I undertake my duties as an usher in the local church, weep with the family over the loss of their daughter, offer words of support to clients who are also present, then go to the drop-in centre, where we sit together in our grief and in our love for each other and drink tea and eat the cake that someone has made for us.

Now, some weeks on, I am greeted by laughter, music and a blur of pink wool. One of the older ladies visiting us is teaching one of the volunteers and a young girl how to knit. Other volunteers are making tea, and I have an overwhelming feeling of thankfulness and love for these people. This is a place of sanctuary. Whatever goes on outside these doors is left outside. It is such a relief to laugh sometimes; it is like a pressure released. This is a solid place among so much that is insecure.

Someone brings me tea in my favourite mug.

Community update

28th August 2013
"The coroner releases the bone fragments known to be April's and the funeral is confirmed as 26 September. National and international press make their way to the small market town of Machynlleth, where a horse drawn carriage has been booked and thousands are expected to line the streets and attend funeral service." (www.bbc.co.uk/news)

On 26th September 2013 the town held its breath again as, at last, after all the waiting, April's family was finally able to hold a funeral service for their beloved daughter. Funerals are events that most of us do not relish attending, but they seem necessary in enabling grievers to mark, and even celebrate, the life of a person who is no longer with them. As Walter points out:

> The purpose of grief is therefore the construction of a durable biography that enables the living to integrate the memory of the dead into their ongoing lives; the process by which this is achieved is principally conversation with others who knew the deceased. The process hinges on talk more than feeling; and the purpose entails moving on with, as well as without, the deceased (Walter 1996, 7).

The funeral was indeed very helpful for many, including those from the wider community; for the family it was, I am sure, not an ending but another step in their painful process of beginning to come to terms with a life without April.

On the day of April's funeral we opened the drop-in during and after the church service to provide a place where volunteers and anyone from the local community could be with others, to talk (or not talk) and sit together over tea and cake. We were at that time all emotionally and physically exhausted. We sat around the table – a clergyman in his robes, volunteers and neighbours clad in pink, and even the police commissioner, in a suit, dropped in, I think not knowing what else to do.

No one was "counselled"; we were dry-eyed, tears long since shed. Someone voices a sense of relief that it was "finally over". We drank tea, ate cake and perhaps felt safe for a while. The anticipation of the event had been terrible in its hold over all of us; it needed to be right for April, for her family, most of us had felt the need to be at the funeral, but had shared how we had dreaded it with every fibre of our beings, our own private losses often triggered by the loss of this child. We spoke little about the funeral. After a while I resumed my needlework; another person brought out her knitting. It was as if the ordinariness of sitting with friends, occupied with ordinary activities, somehow made the dreadfulness of the day bearable.

As an experienced therapeutic practitioner, it interests me that often it was not the counselling service that helped people (including us) in the throes of grieving, or in coming to terms with what had happened on that day in October 2012, but the warmth, laughter and knitting within the drop-in centre.

Maria speaks of the drop-in:

There is a word in the Welsh language that would be instantly recognised and constantly used by any Welsh person the length and breadth of this country.

This word is "cwtsh" and, like many Welsh words that relate in any way to emotion, there is no literal translation and in fact you probably wouldn't find this word in a dictionary or even see it written down – it is part of our spoken language. Some people might say that a cwtsh is a cuddle and that to cwtsh is to cuddle, but that is not enough. A cwtsh is an act of love, not in any way sexual but a special, meaningful embrace that tells a naughty child it's ok now – you are forgiven, you are loved unconditionally. A cwtsh is an act of acceptance; it doesn't matter what you've done or who you are, you belong to us and we care for you.

There is another meaning to the word in the sense that a cwtsh can be a small space – a cubby hole, somewhere to store things of importance, or things that need to be put away for now but you know they are held safe.

I often think that Machynlleth Listening Point should have been called "Y Cwtsh" because that is what we are and that is what we do. Anyone who comes through our door is coming to a place of love and acceptance. If someone needs company, they will find it; they will be welcomed with a smile and a cup of tea. If someone needs to talk, we will listen and will not judge; it is ok to be sad or scared, angry or confused.

When I started volunteering at the Listening Point I felt guilty that I had feelings of terrible grief not only for the people directly involved in the tragic death of April but a more personal grief that arose from a hurt that such a thing could happen in this town, a town where I was born and raised and my children were raised to run about safely and come home when tired or hungry.

I questioned my own parenting skills; should I have watched my own children more closely? Should we have been less trusting? Everything seemed different, even memories of happy events marred by what could have happened – but what right did I have to feel this grief? This is not my tragedy.

The Listening Point drop-in has shown me that not only must we be accepting of other people, we must also be accepting of ourselves; our emotions are important too; sometimes we as volunteers need, and unfailingly receive, comfort and support from each other.

Under the guidance of Sue a group of very different people have come together to create a special place: a place to be held physically, or metaphorically; and a place where memories, good or bad, problems and emotions can be taken to be stored safely and confidentially.

When I walk around the corner and see our little blue building I feel an immediate sense of peace and an easing of everyday stresses and if we can pass that on to those who walk through the door we have succeeded in what we have set out to do.

Where does therapy happen?

To my surprise much of the therapeutic work of Listening Point took place not within the confines of the counselling room (although that was also well used) but within the drop-in sessions. As discussed earlier, the project encompassed a confidential counselling service, telephone helpline and a twice-weekly drop-in centre. When the project started, the drop-in was set out café style, with tables and chairs and a private room set aside, we thought, for those wanting to talk about difficult feelings. What happened time and time again, however, was that the private room remained empty and people drew chairs around a central table, with tea (I cannot begin to calculate how many cups we made over the course of the project). Some knitted or sewed, others did jigsaws; some just chatted about the ordinary and everyday happenings that made up their lives.

There seemed to be something very important about being together, even through the terrible times; being free in this space to be normal, to cry, to laugh, to hug each other, to talk about what was going on around us, but also to talk about the other joys and griefs we encountered in our daily lives. It was a space where it was possible to feel "normal" in a time where everything that we valued and thought we knew seemed changed. There seemed to be little distinction between those of us attending as "volunteers" and those who were "service-users"; we were all enmeshed within the unfolding tragedy. The ground rules pinned to the wall stated "Whatever is said in the drop-in stays in the drop-in" and the core conditions of acceptance, non-judgement and unconditional positive regard (Rogers 1961) enabled us to remain open to whoever, or whatever, came through the door. It was ok to say "April's Garden is the one place I feel peace" or "I hate seeing the garden as it reminds me constantly of what happened to her." It was ok to be angry, happy or sad, or just fed up.

Much counselling research now concludes that it is the quality of the therapeutic relationship that determines the outcomes of the therapeutic process, rather than the kind of therapy offered (Feltham and Horton 2000). This relationship is founded on the core conditions that Carl Rogers identified as non-judgemental positive regard, acceptance and empathy (Rogers 1978). This was the philosophy of the centre – although it was not always easy to maintain these principles. (It was especially hard when Alun Gibbard, the author of the book *Pink Ribbons for April,* came to interview us. Hostility emanated from every pore of our being – he was writing about us, not with us, and this publication felt 'too early' and was "trying to sensationalise" or gain author acclaim. When it was published on 1 October 2013, exactly one year after April's death, many copies were sold outside the area, but many unsold copies lined the shelves of local shops, and some volunteers and visitors reported feeling sick even looking at the cover, let alone opening it.)

From the time that April went missing, many in the community, for a variety of different reasons, appeared to present with symptoms of trauma. Sometimes these were triggered when childhood or other traumatic events surfaced as April's story unfolded and touched people in unexpected ways. A visitor from the US told me: "My daughter died when she was the same age as April. I just cannot stop crying. I wake up in the night with flashbacks from that time."

Others found the images the unfolding drama brought to mind totally unbearable. The constant press coverage meant that, however we were feeling, we were all bombarded with gruesome details, while the media monitored our reaction. We were under constant scrutiny and Machynlleth, like many places, is a place where privacy is valued and dirty washing is not hung outside to dry. A young woman told me at the beginning of the project, "We don't tell our problems here, I doubt if anyone will come to see your counsellors." Certainly fewer people accessed the "counselling service" than we expected; however, the opportunity offered by the drop-in to be alongside others was appreciated. As Paidraig Ò Tuama, a poet involved with reconciliation work in Belfast, comments of his work there:

> There is an Irish saying that, rendered in English, is 'It is in the shelter of each other that the people live.' The saying in Irish is 'Ar scáth a cheile a mhaireas na daoine.'

He goes on to explore his work with groups of Catholics and Protestants:

> The rooms where we gathered were always warm, and we never sat in an open circle. We always sat around tables that were populated with safety – tea, coffee, milk, sugar, pots, biscuits and half-eaten sandwiches. Why this populated space? Because it's ordinary; because it echoes the tables we sit

> at in our own homes; because too much empty space has been our problem, not our solution. There have been too many lives lost and too many stories blanked (Ò Tuama 2014, 14).

There is something very powerful about "standing alongside" one another; the ordinariness of drinking tea together that filled the empty space left by April's death and the loss of the safe boundaries relating to community life. This shared space enabled a new kind of narrative to emerge: a narrative outside the one being played out all around us.

Narrative views of standing alongside

In my view, one of the helpful stances of narrative therapy is the consideration that we socially construct reality through relationship and the stories we tell (White 2007a). Narrative therapists encourage people to look beyond the problem-saturated stories that dominate their lives towards "rich full descriptions" that seek exceptions and build realities that are "more than" the problem. This does not mean ignoring the pain another person feels, or not bearing witness to their accounts, but it does mean trying to find ways of re-connecting also with other different stories that make people stronger. A precursor to this narrative therapy practice and a good example of this would be to consider the work of social anthropologist Barbara Myerhoff, who enabled an elderly, isolated Jewish community in America to reconnect with stories from their lives that resonated with others, thereby helping them to reconstruct their shared history. These "definitional ceremonies", allowed one person's story to be witnessed by others and they in turn told stories of their own lives. Through this telling and witnessing participants began to re-define themselves as distinct from the problem-saturated stories of isolation and loneliness in their current lives. (For more information about the work of Myerhoff and definitional ceremony (Myerhoff 1979, 1982, 1986; White 2007a; Dale 2010, 2011, 2013).

Narrative therapists Michael White and David Epston developed these ideas for therapeutic use in family therapy in Australia. They incorporated definitional ceremonies and outsider witness practices to enable clients who felt marginalised and isolated to connect with other people's stories and, out of that connection, find new stories by which to define their oown lives (White and Epston 1990). Narrative therapists also listen carefully to what is said, but also look for unique outcomes, or for elements that are absent from the person's telling of the story but implicit in their lives (White 2007a). Michael White writes:

> Although life is rich in lived experience, we give meaning to very little of this experience. The aspects of lived experience that are rendered meaningful are those that we take into the known and familiar storylines of our lives; these aspects are highly selected. The myriad experiences of daily life mostly pass like a blip across the screen of our consciousness and into a historical vacuum. Many of these experiences are "out of phase" with the plots or themes of the dominant stories of our lives and thus are not registered or given meaning to. However, these out-of-phase aspects of lived experience can provide a point of entry for the development of alternative storylines of people's lives (White 2007a, 219).

Overnight on 1st October 2012 Machynlleth became the community where April Jones was abducted. The Welsh market town, with its beautiful hillsides and many other traditions, the thriving centre of local creativity and hospitality to visitors was lost. The long police search and constant police presence; the grief, shock and horror of the unfolding story meant that, for many of us, this is what filled our world, and shaped other people's perception of us. Television and radio news broadcasts and the sound of helicopters became the dominant aspect of our existence. For many months afterwards, if I told anyone I lived in Machynlleth, the response would be similar to that of a taxi driver I met in London: "That's where little April went missing… That is so terrible…"

The community had been depicted by the press as one entity standing beside a grieving family. And indeed the people in Machynlleth were remarkable in their response, and have continued to be remarkable, and this standing together was indeed helpful in that it enabled us to avoid isolation; to link our lives, not just around tragedy but with stories of hope, of not giving up, of working together to find a missing child. Not being able to go out searching was, as one elderly lady told me, "even more terrible" than being able to do something to help.

The community efforts are evident, even in the press archives. During the early days of the searching people were able to join with each other, share their feelings and, through this, support one another. There was a common aim. For example, the morning after April went missing teams of people were producing flyers showing her picture asking "Have you seen April?" Volunteers stood at road junctions handing them out and running from place to place. Towards the end of the day I observed a group of tired volunteers physically supporting each other as they made their weary way home. As time went on, however, and the police took over the searching, there were fewer opportunities to be together and to share; the police support officers noted a general feeling of helplessness within the community, which was why they encouraged the setting up of some kind of support service. In the light of the media image of the community, and the genuine compassion for the family at the centre of the tragedy, it was even more difficult to respond individually, outside what was perceived as "the norm". Visitors to the centre told a different stories, with comments ranging from "I felt guilty laughing, or going to the shops," and "I felt angry" to "I just want to get back to normal," and "I am so glad that it was not my child." Without the ability to say what they felt out loud, there might have been a sense of isolation and even guilt.

Research has shown survivor guilt to be prevalent within communities where a traumatic event has occurred. Hodgkinson and Stewart, in *Coping with catastrophe: A Handbook of Post-Disaster Psychological Aftercare*, comment:

> For the survivor, the encounter inevitably involves a corruption of innocence. Once something of this nature has happened to a person, it is very difficult for them to believe that life can ever be the same again; that they can let their children walk across the street (Hodgkinson and Stewart 1991, 2).

In Machynlleth parents became afraid for their children; children awoke in the night with fears about "what happens if someone takes me?" The enduring image for me is seeing a young mother at the 2012 lantern procession with tears streaming down her face as she held her child close while he struggled to join in the procession.

Meeting informally at the drop-in and just talking about "normal things" and laughing with each other, even on one occasion demonstrating Welsh folk dancing, enabled a deep bond to form between us, and for an alternative stories to emerge. Those alternative stories did not dispute the pain and horror of the events, but it gave those present a safe place and a community base from which to continue their lives.

Strangely, there were many who wanted to support the project and commented "I am so glad you are there," but did not attend the drop-in or counselling service or ring the helpline. There seemed something very powerful and even therapeutic about "knowing we were there". One local lady commented, "When I walk past the centre and see the press camped out in the car park I think 'YES'. It is like an act of compassion, yet defiance, it is really important." When I invited her to join us for a cup of tea, her response was, "When I need to come, I will. For now it is enough to know you are there." These sentiments were echoed many times over the months that followed.

Creativity

We were very fortunate to have, as one of our volunteers, an art therapist, who ran a number of family creativity workshops. These were well attended and enabled all ages to engage in a number of different creative projects, such as silk screen printing and creating books of their life experiences.

This work was not formally "art therapy" but it was "therapeutic art", and it embraced many informal creative activities. We all tried things that in other settings we would have never thought about.

I am often asked what the point of creative methods are when it comes to therapeutic interventions. It seems easy to demonstrate to people (through creative exercises) what the point of creativity is in this context, but to write about it seems more challenging. Perhaps this is because, as Pearson points out in her book about creativity and counselling:

> This book considers creative processes; that is, it explores intuitive non-linear processes – activities governed by the *right* side of the brain. Yet committing them to paper requires verbal expression – a process carried out by the left side of my brain. Effectively, then, I [am] trying to force right side of brain activity into *left* side of brain expression. (Pearson 1994, 4).

It is like trying to translate from one language to another.

There are some conundrums in life that, however hard we "think through them" using our intellect, we cannot solve them; the process just leads to more questions. Shel Siverstein (2006) writes:

> I asked the zebra,
> Are you black with white stripes?
> Or white with black stripes?
> And the zebra asked me,
> Are you good with bad habits?
> Or are you bad with good habits?
> Are you noisy with quiet times?
> Or are you quiet with noisy times?

Are you happy with some sad days?
Or are you sad with some happy days?
Are you neat with some sloppy ways?
Or are you sloppy with some neat ways?
And on and on and on and on
And on and on he went.
I'll never ask a zebra
About stripes
Again.

Rather like the zebra question, however much we question why April was abducted and murdered, and why Mark Bridger committed such a dreadful crime, we cannot find an answer, only more stripes.

For example, I remember talking with a young person about what had helped him during what had been a really difficult time. He could not think of an answer. However later, when drawing a picture about a recent visit to a safari park, he drew a beautiful zebra (which brought the poem above to mind). I did not have to ask him whether it was black with white stripes, or white with black, the answer was obvious – it was yellow (he started with yellow), with purple stripes. Yellow because the zebra was in this young person's view a "cheerful" character; purple stripes because black was too boring a colour for an animal that "danced" the way he had seen them do at the safari park, which was, apparently, "how I am when I play football with my friends".

The stones painted by the children (and some adults) for April's Garden and the glorious knitting on the "hugging tree" in Machynlleth said so much more, and gave a much more coherent reply to questions about "How do you feel about this?" than any of the answers we could have given in writing. It showed people's love for a vibrant, smiling little girl and their care for her family.

I have often seen, as a therapist, the transformation as someone moves from describing their situation within the confines of "prose" to describing it through art, metaphor, drama and music. One young visitor at the drop-in said very little but always came and created for us art and needlework that brightened our walls.

As well as using creative methods to explore our thoughts, feelings and behaviour, we can also use creative means as an escape – a means to focus our minds on something other than what is causing us pain and anxiety. People who brought anxiety to the drop-in would often pick up knitting, a jigsaw, or join me as I made patchwork squares. Some brought their own exquisite needlework. The “doing” of something with our hands as we talked allowed tension to slip away and took away the need to always have something to say.

Outside the remit of the project, local knitters also created the “knitting” or “hugging” tree. The tree stood on the hillside, bedecked in pink knitting and a visible demonstration of the values, love and support of people who cared so much about children, family and April.

As well as the impromptu art and creativity that happened within the drop-in centre, we also offered on a number of occasions a creative space to local children. This included painting stones that could be put on April’s Garden, which expanded when local mothers took it on and provided tables on the central green space and many more paints and stones so that more children and young people could be involved. It felt very satisfying to see how an idea from the centre was picked up and developed by members of the community.

Considerations and conclusions

- Having a space where we could be together, and be accepted for whoever we were and however we felt, was extremely therapeutic, but challenging to manage when too many opposing viewpoints presented at the same time or we volunteers (who were also affected by the issues) felt very differently from the person expressing the view.

- There was within the drop-in little difference between the volunteers and the visitors to the centre. On the whole people felt more comfortable about being a “volunteer” than they did about being a “visitor”. The regular meetings, training and sharing of lives was experienced as therapeutic.

- Informal creative arts activities enabled people to express thoughts and feelings that they felt unable to put into words, or gave them something to do while they enjoyed the safe space within the drop-in, or enabled us to be present with each other without the stress of always having to say something. It was also possible to lose yourself in the creative act so there was no time to think about anything else –a kind of escapism that was necessary for many, from time to time.

- Having a "centre of normality" amid the tragedy and chaos into which we had been flung felt important to all of us. Potential visitors might not have wanted to be seen to be "needing help", or to acknowledge the vulnerability that comes from being "helped". Most of us feel much more comfortable with being in a helper role. What we found was that if people came to knit or do a jigsaw or to bring us some donated item, the talking and sharing happened anyway.

- People from outside the area often visited us and expressed surprise at what they found. Many said they came expecting "lots of tears, angst and stress" and what they found was laughter, conversation and friendship.

CHAPTER FOURTEEN

SETTING UP SERVICES FOR COMMUNITIES AFFECTED BY TRAUMATIC EVENTS

General comments

Each chapter has included some considerations and conclusions about the Listening Point project and what it offered. This chapter goes on to make basic recommendations based on the outcomes from the project and our observations. The following points are offered as issues that you may wish to take into consideration should you decide to set up some kind of support service in the wake of a traumatic community event. They are not meant to be prescriptive. Of course, each community will be different, and each particular situation will be unique.

Talk to community leaders and any police team co-ordinators, to ensure their support for the service that you are planning; it is important that what you are offering does not replicate anything else already in place, or that is planned, and that it enhances existing provision.

Working alongside and using existing community expertise and resources is key, as is gaining the support of any police teams. In Machynlleth, for example, we found that the police teams were very helpful with negotiating with the press on our behalf, and our regular meetings with the police liaison officers meant we had a good understanding of the unfolding investigation and the trial, and they could liaise, where necessary, with April's family and keep them updated on what we were doing. Community police teams often visited the drop-in and it helped them to begin to make relationships with the wider community on the Bryn-y-Gog estate and in Machynlleth.

Think carefully about who has the relevant skills to oversee and run your project, and remember that if you wish to raise funds or rent a premises you will need to have charitable status. You could, as we were able to do, ask an existing charity (offering counselling or bereavement support) to host your initiative. This will have many advantages in terms of providing you with charitable status and existing protocols and procedures, but we found that a dynamic project responding to a traumatic event needed different procedures and greater flexibility, and this sometimes caused conflict with the slow-moving committee structure of our host charity.

If you are going to rely on volunteers, consider how much you can reasonably ask them to do, how you will pay their expenses, and who will be their line manager or point of contact. Ensure you share the organisational burden: when key volunteers left Listening Point, my workload doubled, and I was also a volunteer.

Where will the funding, insurance and the governance come from to ensure your project runs safely? Any support project may need to be sustained over a long period of time – months rather than weeks, and certainly long after the initial enthusiasm to "help" has passed. It will also need to comply with any legal obligations and, if including therapeutic work, an ethical framework or ethical code of practice, and clear guidance on how to work with potential witnesses who might have to give evidence in a trial.

How will you advertise what you do? It is essential that people know that your service exists. Despite house-to-house distribution of flyers and posters put up around the town and in places like the GP surgery and the library, people still arrived at the drop-in saying "I didn't know you were here until my GP referred me." In retrospect, it would have been helpful to have someone on the team who had good marketing skills.

If you are hoping that the service will offer a therapeutic element, how will you ensure that what you offer is helpful? Counselling, Egan tells us, will always change things, either for the better or for the worse (Egan 1990). It is important if you are working with people who are already traumatised that the change is for the better. It is now commonly recognised that people can be re-traumatised through being asked ineptly about their traumatic experiences (Van der Kolk, McFarlane, and Weisaeth 1996). So make sure you have someone leading the project who has training and skills in working with trauma.

Helpline

Think carefully about who will staff your helpline and when it will be available for people to call. We found that using trained, experienced counsellors for this purpose meant we could signpost and refer callers on to counselling, whether provided by us or externally, more appropriately, and the counsellors were able to manage the more emotional calls, which often came from people who were deeply distressed by unfolding events.

When the project entered its second year the helpline became more of a counselling referral line, and fewer people phoned to talk about "how they felt" at that moment. This meant that one of the volunteer listeners was able to field many of the calls when they came in on the Listening Point landline.

As a charity, we were classed by the telephone companies as a business; our telephone charges were, therefore, more expensive, and we had to agree to a longer contract for service than if we had a residential line. We opted to have a 0845 number, but most people (apart from the media) contacted us on our landline. We decided that, as most of our calls were going to be lengthy, we could not afford an 0800 number, which would have been free for callers but we would have had to pay a much higher charge per minute for each call received.

Being able to transfer calls to a mobile proved very useful and enabled us to share the workload when the helpline was especially busy. It is worth remembering, however, the difficulties with maintaining confidentiality on a mobile (for example, when taking calls in locations where confidentiality cannot be guaranteed).

Drop-in

Much has been written about the drop-in in this book, as this was the area where most of the volunteers were engaged, and was the most proactive and busy.

The main points drawn out in the preceding chapters are:

- Where the drop-in centre is located is key. Too far out and people will not be able to come; too close to the centre of action/interest, and the media will also swiftly drop in!

- A relaxed, light atmosphere was needed to put people at their ease. Many cam to Listening Point to escape from the awfulness of what was going on outside.

- Wool, knitting needles, paper, jig-saws, pens and basic art equipment are important. A lot of the talking happened while volunteers and visitors knitted, sewed and did jigsaws.

- Being located in an overtly religious setting can be off-putting for some.

- It is essential to support volunteers with training and supervision, and to understand and meet their needs. It is also important to identify and be explicit about what you want of them. I recognise that it was unreasonable to expect expert volunteers to give more of their time than they felt able to.

- Tea, coffee, cakes and biscuits were very much part of what we offered at the drop-in, and to provide them we needed to be inspected for health and hygiene (for which we were awarded five stars)

- It is essential to establish clear referral routes for emergencies or referrals to counselling, mental health or other services.

- Agree and enforce basic ground rules. In Machynlleth we opted to put menus on all tables that described all the services we offered and also stated the ground rule, "What is said in the drop-in stays in the drop-in". This was also displayed on the wall, with the insurance and hygiene certificates and details of the BACP Ethical Framework that underpinned our work.

- At Listening Point, our policy was to have two people on duty at the drop-in, one with counselling experience and at least one other volunteer – in practice most volunteers came to most sessions. This enabled us to provide one-to-one support if anyone needed it, without leaving the drop-in unstaffed.

- Our good relationship with the police ensured that the international media kept their distance.

Counselling service

Counselling and psychotherapy are very skilled activities and should only be undertaken by practitioners with the relevant professional training and supervision. Further information about counselling can be found on the BACP website at www.bacp.co.uk. The following are just some of our observations in respect of the counselling service.

Ensure that suitable protocols and procedures are in place, including clear safeguarding, child protection and confidentiality policies, and referral routes.

If you are going to use volunteer counsellors, you need to have experienced supervisors and managers. This is because volunteer counsellors are normally trainees with little experience and, although very enthusiastic and committed to providing a professional service, they may need back up on occasion.

If you are going to run the counselling service from the same venue as your drop-in, then think about the practicalities: how are you going to protect the privacy of the counselling clients who may not wish to be observed using the service? If, as we did in Machynlleth, you decide to operate the counselling service on a different day or time from the drop-in, there may be other issues: for example, if people saw that someone was in the centre, they came in, so you will need to consider whether it is good practice for your counsellor to be alone in the building with a client. At Listening Point there was always one of us in the building (often attending to office work) when the counsellor was working. This ensured people arriving early, or dropping in (despite it not being a drop-in day), or even other visitors such as the local police, could be welcomed without disruption to the counselling session.

CHAPTER FIFTEEN

ETHICAL CONSIDERATIONS

Working within a therapeutic, then research, project as dynamic as Listening Point brought many ethical dilemmas and questions about how best to respond to the diverse needs of both the volunteers and the wider community. For example, heightened emotions led to tensions over the media's presence: some welcomed them, seeing it as important that April remained in the news and other people's thoughts; others found their presence almost intolerable. Another example was April's Garden, which was seen by some as a "healing space" but by others as "just a reminder of all the awful things that have happened".

Dual relationships emerged where we were both "of the community" and "for the community". We sometimes saw different people from the same families who all had different needs, or neighbours with differing opinions.

Police shared information with us relating to the investigation, and we also from time to time saw individuals who would, or could, be called as witnesses in the impending trial. This meant that we had to remain aware of whether any disclosure might have an impact on the course of the police investigation, for example, many parents were anxious in case their children had been photographed or had contact with Mark Bridger. We needed to be careful not to compromise the trial in any way. For example, if we were working with a potential witness, it was important to keep in mind the guidance given by the Crown Prosecution Service in respect of vulnerable witnesses and therapy. You can download a really helpful guide directly from the Crown Prosecution Service website at: www.cps.gov.uk /publications/prosecution/pretrialadult.html. Further helpful guidance can also be found within Bond and Sandhu's book *Therapists in Court: Providing evidence and supporting witnesses.* (Bond and Sandhu, 2005) The authors hear make the point when working with child witnesses that "Discussion about the content of evidence prior to a trial may give rise to questions about the validity of the child's memory" (p 83). I was well aware throughout the lead up to the trial, that one of the key witnesses to April's abduction was a very young child, and that other children had also been out playing with April that evening.

It was important to all of us, whatever our feelings, that Mark Bridger received a fair trial.

It was very important to develop a clear ethical decision-making model to guide us in our work. We turned to the ethical principles and values set out in BACP's Ethical Framework (BACP 2013). For example, if a dilemma occurred in respect of breaching client confidentiality, we considered the level of the risk, who was at risk, what ethical principle or value might be the most important factor, what legal responsibilities we might have (for example, disclosure of harm to a child), who might be affected if we breached confidentiality and what the consequences could be.

We made decisions, wherever possible, in consultation with each other, and in consultation with our independent supervisors. I have developed a checklist for my own use. Working through this list in an orderly way ensures my decisions are rational and consistent, rather than a more emotive "knee jerk reaction". This, I consider, helped us to ensure all of our therapeutic services stood on strong ethical foundations.

BACP's newly-updated *Ethical Framework for the Counselling Professions* (BACP, 2015) (http://www.bacp.co.uk/ethical_framework/) has the same values and principles of earlier versions, but now starts with six commitments to clients. I wish it had been available while Listening Point was open as I think it describes accurately, and in simple language, how we approached all of our work and the people who accessed our services. These were commitments to: put clients first, work to professional standards, show respect, build appropriate relationships with clients, maintain integrity and demonstrate accountability and candour. The document can be accessed in full at: www.bacp.co.uk/ethics/EffCP.php.

The research process that has underpinned this publication has, in addition to these commitments, values and principles, taken into consideration Bond's recommendations in *Standards and Ethics for Research in Counselling and Psychotherapy* (Bond 2004).

As discussed earlier, the research documented in this book has been collaborative, and therefore ethical decision-making has been a group effort, and it has enabled, I hope, co-researchers to make informed decisions about what they share and how this information was presented and the consequences of publishing it, not only for themselves but also for their families and their work.

CHAPTER SIXTEEN

ENDINGS

"Among my people, questions are often answered with stories. The first story almost always evokes another, which summons another, until the answer to the question has become several stories long. A sequence of tales is thought to offer broader and deeper insight than a single story alone" (Pinkola Estes 1993).

Sue's journal: 1st October 2014

Echo in the bones
Two years after those events I text my former colleagues and friends in Machynlleth; the sound of a helicopter flying overhead in Lutterworth, where I am working, has momentarily transported me back to October 1st 2012. I feel the same fear; a deep pain; the knowledge that nothing will ever be the same again. I have a sudden urge to weep. Volunteer Ceri responds, texting: "once the cushioning effect of shock has gone the pain comes more deeply into the body." I smile. Ceri, so still and so empathic, her intimate knowledge of the pain of loss informing us all. We cannot know what April's family experience; for myself and Ceri,, the onlookers, the pain is indeed still there, but changed. The trauma that affected our small community has become embodied; it has moved from the cognitive and surface feelings to an echo in our bones – an echo as painful as rheumatic joints on a damp day. The events of that first week in October 2012 have marked us all.

Currently most of the residents of Machynlleth give the appearance that they have resumed their lives and everything is normal. For the family of April I guess it is very different, but to the casual observer children play in the parks again, tourists visit, and events and festivals show the fullness of life here in these beautiful Welsh valleys. People no longer want to talk about what happened here two years ago, and rightly they are looking forward. There is talk of a new bridge to cross the river Dyfi (the current one regularly floods), the market bustles with life, as does the newly refurbished co-operative supermarket. 'We are getting there,' says a friend. Getting where, I wonder?

When the Listening Point project started, I thought it would run for six months, probably until April had been found or the police investigation had ceased. I saw it as providing temporary emotional support to a community at a specific time and that it would have a neat ending, when I and the other volunteers would resume our everyday lives.

As time passed, however, it became evident that this neat ending (that I and so many of my counselling colleagues would have preferred) was not going to happen. What happened in practice was much more messy, in that the project changed and developed, and we changed and became different through the project. It ran for two years, offering differing levels of support according to need at that specific time. People volunteering and those using the services gradually drifted away as their needs changed. By late summer 2014 the drop-in service had become a very small group; the counselling service was still active, but with no forward funding, and we felt that, two years on, different initiatives were needed to support the community; initiatives that did not necessarily define themselves in terms of April's abduction and murder.

Endings at the drop-in – Listening Point

In the autumn of 2014 we met for the last time at the drop-in in the Listening Point centre. We invited many of those who had supported and attended, both as volunteers and as service users. Along with the cake, tea and feasting, we included an exercise to help us reflect on the project and what it meant to us. We shared these responses by writing them on sheets of coloured paper cut into the shape of leaves and placing them on a wall hanging of a tree brought in for the occasion.

These are some of the reflections and responses shared on that day, again presented as a collective voice:

Sue: There has been a lot of laughter at the drop-in. Let's write on yellow oak leaves some of the things that made us smile.

That time I dismantled the jigsaw so that we could turn the tablecloth over.
M's naughty wit (especially concerning handsome police officers)!
Unguarded honest tongues in moments of relaxation.
Learning to knit.

A's stories...
The volunteers.

All the ladies constantly laughing – it is infectious.
Laughing at me saying "I cared", as long as I was paid for it!
This company always makes me laugh.

Maria demonstrating Welsh dancing!
Just Maria!

Laughter seemed a very important part of what we did here; for me it was liberating, freeing and released all the other tensions of my life.

You're very shiny and positive people. That is what makes me laugh and smile :) Thank you.

Sue: Reluctantly perhaps, let's now share on the pink tear-shaped leaves some of the times when we felt sad here in the drop-in.

The reason we were here.
The circumstances that brought us all together.

For a few weeks in Spring 2013 I wasn't sure whether I was
a volunteer or a service user, but you helped me.

I moved to the UK, I left my country, my job, colleagues, friends.
I miss them all.

April's mum bringing bin bags with April's toys
ready to go to the charity shop.

Seeing April's coffin leaving from Bryn-y-Gog.
The day of April's funeral.

Clients – and the Listening Point's embrace.

A little boy painting a stone with April's pink bicycle, because he missed her.

I couldn't help them with this.

Some of the early debriefing exercises
and the trauma workshop.

Going into April's family's house and seeing
the sitting room full of pink balloons.

Sue: Now think about what it is you are going to take away with you from Listening Point, and write it on a new green leaf.

Knowing that working together as a team makes such a difference.

Friendship.
New friends and amazing experiences!

That this started a brilliant facility for the town.

The value of having craft materials.

That I know these people, and they are part of my life – friends.
Really good friends – a sense of community.

The thought that we'll be meeting again – just 'cos we want to!
Knowing these people.

To have membership of a small caring community.
Support and reassurance that is offered by sincere and mindful people.

The camaraderie and friendship.

A spiritual kind of peace.

The inspiration to start knitting.
Friendship, inspiration, positive thinking and positive laughing.

Community, mutual support.

Friendship and compassion.
Positivity and friendliness.

It does not feel like the end, but the beginning of something new, a new page in the book.

Letting me make things, and being kind.

That you have been a beacon of hope in a dark time,
grown from love and care x

Sue's journal: September 2014
We had leaves to give each other with special messages on just for them. I will treasure those given to me, always.

Then, in good Listening Point tradition, we had copious amounts of cake and tea, and continued to laugh and talk. Walking away will be hard, but we walk with each other, and with the knowledge that, following autumn and winter, new leaves grow on the tree we have grown together; and what a tree!

Post-Autumn 2014

To an extent researching and writing about the project has been an extension of Listening Point. We have met, collaborated, and drunk more tea together, but we recognise that we have also moved on, beyond the confines of Listening Point. We have friendships that go beyond any project or particular series of events. We take new skills and knowledge with us, and we are now scattered to the wind in our different work and social and family lives. I ask the co-researchers to say a little more about how they view the ending of Listening Point now, in Autumn 2015.

Hope writes:

Endings are like beginnings for me, a tricky place to be. They make me want to check and recheck my emotional anchors, check that all my familiar things are still the same. That is, my husband, children, grandchild and friends are constant. For April's parents that would never be possible in the same way again and I felt very sorry about that.

At the end of the Listening point I think I felt the loss all over again: the loss of April, the loss of a safe community, the loss of that little part of life that had been so normal, so taken for granted, in our small community. I remember my heart aching, like many of my painful past endings.

It felt helpful for me to remember past happy times, problems listened to, problems shared, a sense of being useful in this crisis. To see April's parents taking positive actions in the media to make sense of their pain. To remember Mark Bridger and the justice done, safely locked away, never to cause harm again, a distant and contained figure.

What of me in all this? I feel enriched by my experiences, a personal journey in a public crisis. I have made some wonderful friends and touched the boundaries of my own experiencing; feelings that surprised me with their strength and ferocity, their depth and their rawness. I felt like the Listening Point lasted for years, but flashed by in a second, too fast for me to really grasp. But I have no regrets, only memories, pains and pleasures, and a special place in my heart.

Lisa writes:

Endings are always a funny thing! Endings always mean change, for good or bad. As humans generally, we don't like change. In certain situations it is sometimes healthier to end something sooner rather than later, before it fizzles out in a negative way.

The ending of Listening Point was inevitable at some point. It had served the purpose it had been set up for. We had been there for the community of Machynlleth for two years. Time now, I felt, for the residents to move on in their own way and in their own strength. I get the feeling some people at the moment would like to try and disassociate Machynlleth from the tragic set of circumstances, although I guess it will always be on the map for what happened.

April will never be forgotten, but we all want to try and forget the monster who committed the most heinous of crimes and the act itself, still too shocking to contemplate. For some there is never an ENDING; April's family have to live and endure that agony day by day to the END of their lives.

It was a day of mixed emotions when Listening Point closed. Two years earlier a group of people had come together from all walks of professional life to form a network of volunteers, opening the doors, and their hearts, to the community of Machynlleth to help and support people in any way they could.

We had a tea party to say our goodbyes to old friends, as we had all become. It was a time to reflect on what had been achieved by this small group of wondrous and special people.

In retrospect I don't feel I would change anything about the process of setting up and running Listening Point.

A group of like-minded people formed to try and help a community in shock and distress. They needed to do something for themselves as well as everyone else in the midst of such a terrible tragedy. We went about that task in the best way we knew how, with our various skill sets. We had to go with what felt right at the time and inch our way forward gently with the deep emotional pain felt in the heart of everyone.

That fog of grief, despair and disbelief that hung suffocatingly in the air. The tension felt by locals as crews of TV cameras and reporters arrived in their drones on every street corner. People walking around like startled deer in the headlights.

Sue Dale did a brave and magnificent job in the handling of this project. She not only supported the community, including the family of April, but also the volunteers and counsellors.

We all learned an awful lot being part of an amazing team. I salute them all.

Other people's views

Emails were often received from people who were local and from others all over the world. Some people came to the drop-in or used the helpline or counselling service; some did not use the services but still supported our activities. These are just a few of the messages received over the two years, and have been included with explicit permission from the correspondents.

> You begin to think that everyone is coping except you! And then when you start talking you realise they are feeling too! Sharing things with others seems to help in a strange way, and you start then talking about things, and finding things that are more positive then.

> What has happened has taken away my world,
> the safety,
> everything I thought I knew of life,
> this place, fairness and justice.
> I look at my daughter and weep.
> You are there though, I might need to come one day.
> Thankyou.

> I don't know what to do
> what to say
> I can't even bear to think of it.
> I sometimes wish it would go away,
> or I could go away,
> I don't know why I email you,
> But thank you for listening.

> Everyone was creeping round the town,
> not looking at anyone
> not smiling.
> Then I came through the door and there was laughter, and warmth and a pretty good cup of tea!

I came to see the garden, but found you instead. Thank you.

It feels really safe here to sit and talk
not necessarily about anything in particular
but to share being with others
where no-one judges you
some people knit
others just sit quiet
sitting alone is too hard some days.

Just thank you. Thank you for being here.

I suppose that I am not really a local
I live here in Mach
but I don't belong here.

Sometimes I feel like a bug that has come in
on the bananas!
accepted, as something "there".
here to stay;
but not really "of" the place.

Locals have been very kind to me –
I've never had any trouble
people always speak in English to me
and are friendly…
You are friendly too. Thank you.

Coming from the outside
I was amazed by how welcoming you all were
Couldn't do enough to help.

I wish I could change things, but I don't want to change your service.

June writes a letter to me about her experiences of being a volunteer at the project and about endings:

> Very gradually professional, funded therapists began to use the centre – very appropriately. Because of the ethos of confidentiality I began to feel placed on the fringe and not really needed any more. Much as I had begun to love the volunteers (who I was coming to know well), I felt it time to move on and put to use the growing care skills I had acquired. I feel I have gained more for myself from the centre than I have been able to give.

I have always hoped that in some small way Listening Point demonstrated an alternative story to the predominant one of tragedy that was being played out in Machynlleth, and that the community's responses and our desire to help in some ways pointed to our strong values and beliefs about children, family and community (White 1999). I also hoped that our writing might show different ways of responding to trauma and the normality of responding with compassion in situations that are portrayed as dreadful.

Lisa writes:

> We hope that you might perceive from reading this book that we can never eradicate the evil in the hearts of mankind; that is for a higher authority. We mere mortals can only dream of making this a perfect world. However, we can continue to believe and trust that, when tragedy strikes, the good in humanity shines forth like a wonderful beacon of hope that continues to shine brightly, filling us with love, peace and friendship, and shows us a way forward through the darkness to achieve our own level of healing.

CHAPTER SEVENTEEN

AN END TO THE WRITING PROCESS

Sue's journal: August 2015

Another ending; a really happy one this time. Somehow there is energy in it, direction, and a really good send off from very good friends.

I am moving next month to Devon, and we are gathered around the teapot in Machynlleth yet again. A gift is given, my tears flow, amongst the laughter and chat; not tears of sadness but of being touched by these people's love and care. I leave with a gift: three teardrops, a reminder that tears are often healing. Everyone talks and laughs; it is so good to see that we are all moving on in such positive ways; not stories of the past today, but stories of hopeful futures, of skills learnt and used and friendships forged through the fire of working together at a time of community crisis.

When the Listening Point closed its doors for the last time, exactly one year ago, there was a mixture of sadness and relief, and possibly, if I am honest, a fear of what might happen next. It did not really feel like an ending where we were ready to move on; rather the closing of one chapter of our lives without knowing, or having the courage to look at, what might happen next.

I worked away from home for a while on a writing project disconnected from Machynlleth. It felt like being in exile yet, in my uncluttered flat in distant Lutterworth, I started one day to think about, and to talk to those who had been involved with, the Listening Point. I remember a colleague in Lutterworth talking with me as we sat and enjoyed a Thai meal together and I realised I could, and in fact I needed to write about the project and explore and ethnographically map carefully my own and others' responses to the murder of April Jones. I knew I could also come home, and that my professional role within Machynlleth was nearly completed.

So the book begins at the end. I am starting a new story, and who knows what Devon will bring! The writing about Machynlleth comes full circle; as TS Eliot reminds us in Four Quartets:

> *"What we call the beginning is often the end*
> *And to make an end is to make a beginning.*
> *The end is where we start from." (Eliot 1943)*

Reflections

Reflecting on the process of researching and writing always seems important, and I am interested to find out what my friends and co-researchers have made of it. For me, it has proved therapeutic, but it has also been the most challenging publication I have ever worked on. It has been extremely, to coin a phrase from Bird, "up close and personal" (Bird 2000). Usually I write autoethnography when therapeutically I have processed the emotions connected with the events. This time, I have processed the emotions while I have written, and that at times has been painful. The stories from co-researchers have swooped backwards and forwards across time, and it has been difficult to pull together the fragmented parts into a coherent account.

What has become apparent, as we have talked and written together, is that to some extent we have all been traumatised, to some extent, by what happened in Machynlleth and that many of our memories of the events were, like many traumatic memories, fragmented pockets of feeling, and not necessarily a historic and contextualised account of what happened in a particular place at a particular time. As we have talked and written together, we have woven these various threads of memories into a coherent narrative that encompasses theoretical models of understanding how we as human beings make sense of our lives. We have produced what Michael White would have described as a "thicker richer description of our preferred reality" (White and Epston 1990). This reality does not in any way take away the devastating loss of April, but it encompasses more than sadness; it relates what one small group of volunteers can, through compassion and determination, achieve. I hope too that, by sharing with others this unique glimpse of lived experience, other communities setting up therapeutic projects may learn from our successes, and failures, and can respond with a small thread, or many threads, of hope.

I ask the contributors what the experience of talking and writing about Listening Point has been like. Hope, the first to respond, writes:

> Writing and talking about the Listening Point project, and what that meant to me in the context of the community trauma we experienced, has been personally a very liberating experience. In respect of my writing contributions, I discovered my writing style; it just came out in a very definite way, a part of me that has been inside, unnoticed, all the time. I am thankful for the "release" because I now write more freely in other areas of my life.
>
> I will admit I had preconceived ideas about what being part of writing this book would be like. A challenging concept for me because I knew how different we volunteers were. And how to write this book? Sue to the rescue; of course you need one person to create the framework on which we could all safely hang our experiences, feelings and emotions.
>
> Once Sue began to share the structure, I realised there was no expectation of quality or quantity. If I felt I had something to contribute, I could ramble away to my heart's content. A little like a closed group supervision session, my contributions were neither right nor wrong. A safe space to explore sometimes controversial feelings and express them freely, as others also expressed emotions freely.
>
> Through this process I have gained clarity of thought and feelings around the April Jones trauma. I didn't believe anything awful like that could happen in Machynlleth, this quiet, safe, little town, but it did. I now have empathy and understanding when I watch the tragic news stories, an insight into what the community goes through.
>
> Writing for this book has also helped me make sense of the press and reporter intrusion that unfolds behind the television screens. It has helped me remember and understand I too am part of that

intrusion every time I watch the news or read a reporter's article. I have a relationship with all of this and began to feel that getting to know this relationship better by writing was my way forward.

Just as the Listening Point project was a safe place to hear the trauma of others and evaluate my own, so the writing for me has deepened this healing process and helped me understand my relationship with the trauma. Each time we met as a group of volunteers to discuss this book and content, I felt myself both identifying with others and then after a while not needing to identify; I felt a change. The feelings I now have are separate from the group, where I had once needed so much comfort and reassurance from that very group. I realised this process has also been, for me, about working through so many other losses and bereavements in my life. I wonder if it's a little like when Princess Diana died: I felt great loss; I can still feel it now, were I was when I heard the news. I have similar feelings and memories about April Jones, but through the writing it's not so raw and difficult to look at; I understand the story.

I feel the talking, sharing and writing process has had a profoundly positive effect on me. I have been fascinated to read research to help me understand the bigger picture. There was a particular article in Psychology Today that really helped me make sense of what was happening. The author basically said our perceptions of traumatic events are disjointed: "You have painful facts with no story to bind them together." Of course! That was part of why I didn't want to think about it.

The writing process has helped me make sense of the trauma, fitting it together while mentally processing the experience. The very act of writing has allowed me to let it go from my mind and see it on the page, separate from me and more manageable. My usual default setting is to avoid painful feelings and let them find a rather uncomfortable shadowy place in my being, to be triggered at any time and relived. A significant amount of time needed to pass before I could start to write my story. I have written my story now and I am thankful.

Writing my story has changed my thoughts about what happened. I feel more compassion and empathy, less judgement and anger; an accepting. It has helped me challenge my fears and find another way to make sense of my vulnerabilities. I have been the creator of a new story full of new perspectives, new beginning and possibilities. It has changed me profoundly and therefore changed my work as a counsellor. Through great pain has come personal growth and learning and I am ever thankful to the love and support of the Listening Point Group and the writing of this book.

Lisa writes:

It appeared very strange and alien at first, attempting to write about the various stages of this journey in a reflective way. As I started to write, it helped in a cathartic way by putting things in the order in which they happened, rather than just a jumbled chaotic nightmare of events.

Personally, it gave me a chance to reflect on where my feelings are today with regards to the atrocity that happened here in Machynlleth, six months after I moved to Wales.

It was painful at times reading the material that had been collated and woven together by Sue. It meant reading it in print, black and white. This really did happen, it was not just a terrible dream or story. It inevitably gave rise to feelings that may have been pushed deep down somewhere, only to be bought once again to the surface feeling open and raw.

Our group meetings were therapeutic because we were given the freedom and opportunity in a safe environment to explore and express our thoughts and feelings that were bubbling to the surface. Deep discussions were chewed over, strong views and still anger regarding the perpetrator were very apparent. Views on forgiveness and rehabilitation, I know, brought forth strong emotion within me. Once I had started to let all this out it felt difficult to stop, a little like a volcano erupting!! It was healthy to unleash these feelings for us all. We could be heard and our words accepted within safe boundaries.

We were also able to discuss the atmosphere within the town of Machynlleth and the community as everybody moved forward in their own way, trying to leave those terrible memories behind. Human nature as we know it always finds ways to criticise other people's ways and reactions with dealing with things. That is 'Life', as we say!!

Postscript

August 2015

Hope: After the ending of the Listening Point, many seasons have passed us by. We have all moved on, we are different because of our experiencing, as we settle back into our lives. Both united and separated, sharing what it means to be human.

Sue: I have been on a quest for answers, and found only stories. These stories have been woven together within a narrative; hopefully a narrative made of threads of hope and resilience and giving inspiration to others and possibilities for further conversations and stories. As Paidraig Ò Tuama writes so eloquently:

Narrative Theology (#1)

And I said to him
Are there answers to all of this?
And he said
The answer is in a story
and the story is being told.

And I said
But there is so much pain
And she answered, plainly,
Pain will happen.

Then I said
Will I ever find meaning?
And they said
You will find meaning
Where you give meaning.

The answer is in the story
And the story isn't finished.

(Ó Tuama 2012. Reprinted by permission)

December 2015

The point of no-return on the final manuscript has been reached; the final decisions on what to include, what not to include. The time also for my co-researchers to decide finally how visible they wish to be in the text. Ó Tuama speaks of a local language he has heard about in Papua New Guinea, where there is no word for "hello"; instead they simply say when someone visits "You are here," and the visitor replies, "I am here" (Ó Tuama 2015, 14).

It is time now for us now to publish, and for readers to say, "You are here." How much, or how we decide to say "I am here" is complicated, and will be dependent on many factors: as authors, by choosing to tell personal stories, we are choosing to make others visible too. I write again to everyone, with a new copy of the updated text, and questions about anonymity or visibility; the response, as usual are more stories.

There are two questions with which I always battle within a narrative process of writing: when have we done enough, and when are the stories finished? The answer, as Pádraig has pointed out in the poem above, is that they are never finished. We continue to make sense of our lives through the telling and the re-telling, and it is through these tellings that some of the pain eases. It is also through the telling and re-telling that the descriptions of who we are and how we are in the world change and become richer and encompass more than the traumatic event.

Ceri responds to my final email with her biography and some further stories:

> Of course a decision has to be made about the starting point, and the ending point, but we all know that in life, within any community crisis, there is the prequel and the sequel and something and someone really made me want to say a little bit about that.
>
> Just the other day, I had watched April's parents on TV earlier that evening talking about a documentary they were involved with about sex offenders who targeted children. They opened the programme with Machynlleth, a shot of Maenwyn Street in the dark!
>
> The programme was very informative. Paul and Coral were amazing in the interview, talking about charity they are working with. What then happened to me on that same evening was a little illustration of how we cannot go back to being who we were before April went missing.
>
> I was just going to a talk at the Y Plas (town hall) when I saw a small girl looking a bit worried and slightly lost. It was dark, even though just before six. I asked her if she was all right and whether her mum was around and she said no she wasn't as she had just been dropped off for "Cubs" but

when she had gone in the room had looked different. I said I would go in with her and ask what was happening. I went in, and saw that the blood donation people were there for one of their occasional outreach services. I asked about the Cubs meeting, but nobody knew anything about it. We then checked other rooms in Y Plas, and, as the girl said the Cubs sometimes went to the next door Leisure Centre, we checked there too, but nobody knew anything.

Then she told me that she didn't know her mum's phone number and didn't have her own phone. She lived out of town and knew that her mum wouldn't be back until 7 to pick her up. As I was going to be in the building where her mum expected her to be, and she looked worried, I made the decision to take her with me to the talk I was going to. I told her it would be very boring, but perhaps better than standing by herself in the rain. She was quite scared and hardly spoke to me and wouldn't even take her coat off in the hot room or accept a biscuit or juice, so clearly obeying instructions about not talking to strangers. I took her down to the car park at 7, although her mother didn't arrive until 7.30pm. Obviously, by then, I had passed some sort of test. She then told me that she went with her mum every Sunday to one of the local churches and asked did I know anyone there. I said, "Yes, I know the vicar," and suddenly she told me everything about her life but she started with asking what were they doing in the Cubs' room "with all those people lying down". Clearly, she had been frightened, seeing the people and the blood, when she walked in expecting to find the Cubs. She spent the next half hour talking about going to the dentist! When her mother arrived I explained I had taken her to a talk on "laughter yoga". I remembered a quotation, which goes something like: "It takes only one mother to give birth, but a whole community to bring up a child." That is what I see as important, something we must take from this, whichever communities we belong to. We as a community are needed to bring up a child.

This was a minor event. I wonder would the little girl have been so frightened prior to what happened to April? Also, would I have been as concerned for her, waiting in the dark street?

APPENDIX 1

STATISTICS FROM LISTENING POINT

2012-2013

Date	Calls to help line	New counselling referrals	Drop-in Visitors	Volunteers Attending drop-in	Training /Activities
Dec-12	4	1 Cruse	Adults 7	8	Cruse training 15
			Children (11-18) 1		Meeting 25
Dec -Total	**4**	**1**	**8**	**8**	**40**
Jan-13	4	1 Relate	Adults 12	18	Meeting 20
			Children (11-18) 1		Listening Skills 11
Jan- total	**4**	**1**	**13**	**18**	**11**
Feb-13	5	1 External counsellor	Adults 23	24	Internal Listening Skills 12
		1 Cruse	Children (11-18) 1		
Feb-total	**5**	**2**	**24**	**24**	**12**
Mar-13	4	1 External counsellor	Adults 21	18	External trainer Trauma 9
			Children 11-18 1		
Mar-total	**4**	**1**	**22**	**18**	**9**
Apr-13	46	2 External counsellor 1 telephone counselling	Adults 43	26	Open Day 62 Volunteers 7
Apr-total	**46**	**3**	**43**	**26**	**69**

May-13	63	5 telephone counselling 5 External counselling	Adults 28	24	Therapeutic Art 6 Volunteers 4
		4 in house counselling			
May-total	**63**	**14**	**28**	**24**	**10**
Jun-13	37	2 in house counselling	Adults 41	26	
			Children 0-5 2		
June 13-total	**37**	**2**	**43**	**26**	**0**
Jul-13	8		Adults 46	26	Fun Day 75 Visitors 8 Volunteers
			Children 0-5 2		Therapeutic Art 6
July 13-total	**8**	**0**	**46**	**26**	**89**
Aug-13	9	2 in house counselling 1 external counsellor	Adults 18	18	
			Children 0-5 2		
			Children 5-11 14		
Aug 13-total	**9**	**2**	**34**	**18**	**0**
Sep-13	20	1 in house counselling	Adults 26	16	Internal training 9
			Children 5-11 3		
			Children 0-5 3		
Sep 13-total	**20**	**1**	**32**	**16**	**9**
Oct-13	16	1 in house counselling	Adults 18-30 2	17	Mindful-ness 10 Volunteers 4
			Adults 30-65 27		Funeral 18 Volunteers 8
			Children 5-11 1		
			Children 0-5 2		
Oct 13-total	**16**	**1**	**30**	**17**	**40**

Nov-13	12	1 in house counselling	Adults 36	17	Therapeutic Art 6 Volunteers 4
			Children 5-11 3		
			Children 0-5 1		
Nov 13-total	**12**	**1**	**39**	**17**	**10**
Dec-13	8	3 in house counselling	Adults 28	17	Christmas Party 28
			Children 5-11 8		
			Children 0-5 3		
Dec 13-total	**8**	**3**	**39**	**17**	**28**
Totals for year	**236**	**32**	**401**	**238**	**327**

Statistics are only provided here for 2012-2013. In January 2014 Listening Point ran a level 1 intensive narrative therapy course attended by both volunteers and other therapeutic workers from within Powys. 18 attendees attained a level 1 certificate. During 2014 there was a gradual reduction in numbers attending the drop-in, and calls to the helpline. The counselling service, however, maintained steady numbers of referrals through to the project's end in September 2014.

Counsellors assessed and assisted clients to complete CORE-IMS outcome measures. For further information about CORE-IMS therapeutic tools to measure outcomes of therapy see http://www.coreims.co.uk. Complete documentation was received from 18 referrals at the close of the project in September 2014 (68% of total referrals – incomplete documentation has not been included).

Outcome measures (taken at the beginning and the end of counselling) enable the client and their practitioner (and service manager) to assess the client's wellbeing, symptoms, functioning and risk. By taking a measurement at the beginning and end of the course of therapeutic sessions the practitioner and client gain a good understanding of what had changed.

From the outcome measure forms collected from the Listening Point in-house counselling service, it was apparent that clients had shown the following changes between referral and discharge:

Wellbeing: 88% improvement
Symptoms: 80% improvement
Functioning: 90% improvement
Risk: 72% improvement

One person was referred on from the counselling service to the Community Mental Health team and two people were referred back to their GP for assessment with regard to medication. Three were referred to specialist agencies (including a local drugs and alcohol project).

REFERENCES

Arulampalam, Shanti., Perera, Lara., de Mel, Sathis., White, Cheryl., and Denborough, David. Stories from Sri Lanka – Responding to the Tsunami. *The International Journal of Narrative Therapy and Community Work: Responding to Trauma Part One.* 2005 2 3-10

Bachelard, Gaston. 1964. *The Poetics of Space.* New York: Orion Press.

BACP. 2013. *The Ethical Framework for Counselling and Psychotherapy.* BACP. Lutterworth: BACP

—. 2015. *BACP Ethical Framework for the Counselling Professions.* Lutterworth: BACP.

Banks, Stephen P., and Anna Banks. 1998. *Fiction and Social Research: By Ice or Fire.* London: Sage.

Behan, Christopher. 2003. *Rescued Speech Poems: Co-Authoring Poetry in Narrative Therapy.* Adelaide: Dulwich Centre Publications. http://www.narrativeapproaches.com/?p=1546

Behar, Ruth. 1997. *The Vulnerable Observer: Anthropology that Breaks Your Heart.* Boston: Beacon Press.

Berthold, S. Megan. 2014. *Vicarious Trauma and Resilience* (2nd edition). NetCE. http://www.NetCE.com

Bird, Johnella. 2000. *The Heart's Narrative: Therapy and Navigating Life's Contradictions.* Auckland: Edge Press.

Bird, Johnella. 2004. *Talk That Sings.* Auckland: Edge Press.

Bonanno, George A. 2004. Loss, Trauma, and Human Resilience: Have We Underestimated the Human Capacity to Thrive After Extremely Aversive Events? *American Psychologist* 59(1):20–28.

Bond, Tim. 2004. *Ethical Guidelines for Researching Counselling and Psychotherapy.* Rugby: British Association of Counselling and Psychotherapy.

Bond, T., Sandhu, A. 2005. *Therapists in Court: Providing Evidence and Supporting Witnesses.* London: Sage Publications.

Burquan, Maryam. 2006. Re-Membering. In *Trauma: Narrative Responses to Traumatic Experience*, edited by David Denborough. Adelaide SA: Dulwich Centre Publications. 174-175..

Carey, Maggie W., Sarah Walther and Shona Russell. 2009. The Absent but Implicit: a Map to Support Therapeutic Enquiry. *Family Process* 48(3): 319–331.

Carroll, Michael. 2011. Supervision: A Journey of Lifelong Learning. In *Supervision as Transformation: A Passion For Learning*, edited by Robin Shohet. London: Jessica Kingsley 14–28.

Cixous, Helene, and Mireille Calle-Gruber. 1997. *Rootprints: memory and life writing*. London: Routledge.

Clandinin, D. Jean, and E. Michael Connelly. 2000. *Narrative Inquiry: Experience and Story in Qualitative Research.* San Fransisco: Jossey-Bass.

Clough, Peter. 2002. *Narratives and fictions in educational research.* Buckingham: Open University Press.

Dabner, Nicki. 2012. Breaking Ground in the Use of Social Media: A Case Study of a University Earthquake Response to Inform Educational Design with Facebook. *The Internet and Higher Education* 15(1): 69–78.

Dale, Susan. 2008. Knitting in the Dark: Narratives about the Experience of Sight Loss in a Counselling Setting. *British Journal of Visual Impairment* September.

—. 2009. The Grilling of Mr B: Using the Narrative Therapy Practice of 'Externalising' Conversations to Co-Research the Experience of Blindness. *Therapy Today* 20(7).

—. 2010. *Where Angels Fear to Tread: Having Conversations about Suicide in a Counselling Context.* Newcastle upon Tyne: Cambridge Scholars Publishing.

—. 2011. *Songs at Twilight: A Narrative Exploration of Living with a Visual Impairment and the Effect this has on Claims to Identity.* Newcastle upon Tyne: Cambridge Scholars Publishing.

—. 2013. *The Secret Keepers: Narrative Approaches to Working with Childhood Sexual Abuse and Violence*. Newcastle: Cambridge Scholars Publications.

Davies, Bronwyn, and Susanne Gannon. 2006. The Practices of Collective Biography. In *Doing Collective Biography*, edited by Bronwyn Davies and Susanne Gannon. Buckingham: Open University Press.

Davies, Bronwyn, and Suzy Dormer, Sue Gannon, Cath Laws, Sharn Rocco, Hillevi Lenz Taguchi, and Helen McCann. 2001. Becoming Schoolgirls: the Ambivalent Process of Subjectification. *Gender and Education* 13(2): 167–182.

Denborough, David, and Carolyn Koolmatrie, Djapirri Mununggirritj, Djuwalpi Marika, WAyne Dhurrkay, and Margaret Yunopingu. 2006. Linking Stories and Initiatives: A Narrative Approach to Working with the Skills and Knowledges of Communities. *International Journal of Narrative Therapy and Community Work* 2: 19-53.

Downing, Melinda, John Rosenthall, and Michele Hudson. 2002. *Community Capacity Building*. WM'02 Conference, February 24–28. Tuscan, AZ.

Egan, Gerard. 1990. *The Skilled Helper* (4th edition). Pacific Grove, California: Brooks/Cole Publishing Company.

Eliot, Thomas S. 1943. Little Gidding. In *Four Quartets* by Thomas S. Eliot. New York: Harcourt.

Elliott, Stuart. 2014. Sabbath Spaces: Losing Control. In *Earthed: Christian Perspectives on Nature Connection*, edited by Bruce Stanley and Steve Hollinghurst. Powys: Mystic Christ Press 132-148.

Etherington, Kim. 2000. *Narrative Approaches to Working with Adult Male Survivors of Child Sexual Abuse.* London: Jessica Kingsley Publishers.

—. 2001. Research with Ex-Clients: A Celebration and Extension of the Therapeutic Process. *British Journal of Guidance and Counselling* 29(1): 5-19..

—. 2007. Ethical Research in Reflexive Relationships. Qualitative Inquiry 13(5): 599-61.

Feltham, Colin and Ian Horton. 2000. *The Sage Handbook of Counselling and Psychotherapy*. London: Sage.

Fussell, Paul. 1983. *Siegried Sassoon's Long Journey*. New York: Oxford University Press.

Gallant, Mike. 2014. Battered Fish Out of Water: a Work in Progress. In *Creative Practitioner Inquiry in the Helping Professions*, edited by Jane Speedy and Jonathan Wyatt. Rotterdam: Sense Publishers.

Haug, Frigga (and others). 1987. *Female Sexualization: A Collective Work of Memory*, translated by Erica Carter. London: Verso.

Hewett, Sandra. 2015. Less Research, More Marketing. Letters. *Therapy Today* 26(1).

Hodgkinson, Peter E. and Michael Stewart. 1991. *Coping with Catastrophe: A Handbook of Disaster Management*. London and New York: Routledge.

Holman, E. Alison, Dana R. Garfin, and Roxanne C. Silver. 2014. Media's Role in Broadcasting Acute Stress Following the Boston Marathon Bombings. *PNAS* 111(1): 93–98.

Houston, Gaie. 1990. *Supervision and Counselling*. London: The Rochester Foundation.

Jemphrey, Ann, and Eileen Berrington. 2000. Surviving the Media: Hillsborough, Dunblane and the Press. *Jouralism Studies* 1(3): 469–483.

Josephs, Jeremy. 1993. *Hungerford: One Man's Massacre*. Edgware: Smith Gryphon.

Karpman, Stephen. 1968. Fairy Tales and Script Drama Analysis. *Transactional Analysis Bulletin* 7(26): 39–43.

Keinan, Giora, Avi Sadeh and Sefi. Rosen. 2003. Attitudes and Reactions to Media Coverage of Terrorist Acts. *Journal of Community Psychology* 31(2): 149–165.

Klass, Dennis, Pyllis R. Silverman, and Steven L. Nickman. 1996. *Continuing Bonds: New Understandings of Grief.* London: Talyor and Francis.

Myerhoff, Barbara. 1979. *Number Our Days*. London. New York: Meridian.

—. 1982. Life History Among the Elderly: Performance, Visibility and Remembering. In *Crack in the Mirror: Reflexive Perspectives in Anthropology*, edited by Joy Ruby. Philadelphia: University of Pennsylvania 99-117.

—. 1986. Life Not Death in Venice: It's Second Life. In *The Anthropology of Experience*, edited by Victor W. Turner and Edward M. Bruner. Chicago: University of Illinois Press.

Naaeke, Anthony., Kurylo, Anastacia., Grabowski, Michael., Linton, David., Radford, Marie. Insider and Outsider Perspective in Ethnographic Research. *Proceedings of the 68th New York State Communication Association. 2010 1 (9.)*.

North, Mick. 2000. *Dunblane: Never Forget*. Edinburgh: Mainstream Publishing (E-Book).

Ò Tuama, Padraig. 2012. *Readings from the Book of Exile*. Norwich: Canterbury Press.

—. 2014. Shelters and Shadows in Belfast. *Thresholds* Autumn.

—. 2015. *In the Shelter: Finding a Home in the World.* London: Hodder and Stoughton.

Parkes, Colin M., and Holly G. Prigerson. 2010. *Bereavement: Studies of Grief in Adult Life*, 4th Edition. Hove: Routledge.

Partington, Marian. 2012. *If You Sit Very Still: A Sister's Fierce Engagement with Traumatic Loss*. Bristol: Vala Publishing Co-operative Ltd.

Pearson, Althea. 1997. *Creative Methods in Counselling: Facilitating the Healing Process*. London: Marshall Pickering.

Pinkola Estes, Clarissa. 1993. *The Gift of Story: A Wise Tale about What is Enough*. London: T. Rider.

Richardson, Laurel. 1990. Writing Strategies; Reaching Diverse Audiences. California: Sage Publications.

Richardson, L. 2000a. Introduction. Assessing Alternative Modes of Qualitative and Ethnographic Research: How Do We Judge? Who Judges? *Qualitative Inquiry* 6(2): 251–252.

Richardson, Laurel. 2000b. Writing: A Method of Inquiry. In *The Sage Handbook of Qualitative Research*, edited by Norman K. Denzien and Yvonna S. Lincoln. London: Sage Publications.

—. 1992. The Consequences of Poetic Representation: Writing the Other, Re-Writing the Self. In *Investigating Subjectivity: Research on Lived Experience*, edited by Carolyn Ellis and Michael Flaherty. Newbury Park, CA: Sage Publications.

—. 2003. Poetic Representation of Interviews. In *Postmodern Interviewing*, edited by Jaber F. Gubrium and James A. Holstein. London: Sage Publications.

Rogers, Carl. 1961. *On Becoming a Person*. London: Constable.

—. 1978. *On Personal Power*. London: Constable.

Rowan, John. 1983. *The Reality Game: A Guide to Humanistic Counselling and Psychotherapy*. London: Routledge.

Salter, Anna C. 1995. *Transforming Trauma: A Guide to Understanding and Treating Adult Survivors of Child Sexual Abuse*. California: Sage Publications.

Sarbin, Theodore R. 2005. If These Walls Could Talk: Places as Stages for Human Drama. *Journal of Constructivist Psychology* 18(3): 203–214.

Shaw, Jackie, and Clive Robertson. 1997. *Participatory Video: A Practical Approach to Using Video Creatively in Group Development Work*. London: Routledge.

Siverstein, Shel. 2006. Zebra Question. In *The Narrative Therapist and the Arts*, 2nd Edition, edited by Pam Dunne. Los Angeles, CA: Possibilities Press.1.

Skodol, Andrew E. 2010. The Resilient Personality. In *Handbook of Adult Resilience*, edited by John W. Reich, Alex J. Zautra and John Stuart-Hall. London: The Guilford Press.

Smith, Brian G. 2010. Socially Distributing Public Relations: Twitter, Haiti and Interactivity in Social Media. *Public Relations Review* 36(4): 329–335.

Speedy, Jane. 2005. Collective Biography Practices: Collective Writing with the Unassuming Geeks Group. *British Journal of Psychotherapy Integration* 2(2): 29–38.

—. 2007. Creating and Performing Autoethnographies: Some Unfortunate Lapses – A Very Short Story. In *Narrative Inquiry and Psychotherapy*, edited by Jane Speedy. Houndsmill: Palgrave Macmillan 112–125.

Speedy, Jane, and Jonathan Wyatt. 2014a. *Collaborative Writing as Inquiry*. Newcastle: Cambridge Scholars Publishing.

Speedy, Jane, and Jonathan Wyatt. 2014b. *Creative Practitioner Inquiry in the Helping Professions*. Rotterdam: Sense.

Spiegel, David. 1991. Trauma and Dissociation. In *American Psychiatric Press Review of Psychiatry Volume 10*, edited by Allan Tasman. New York: American Psychiatric Press.

Tedlock, Dennis. 1983. *The Spoken Word and the Work of Interpretation.* Philadelphia: University of Pensylvania.

Terr, Lenore. 1991. Childhood Traumas: An Outline and Overview. *American Journal of Psychiatry* 148(1): 10–20.

Van der Kolk, Bessel A., Alexander C. McFarlane, and Lars Weisaeth (Eds). 1996. *Traumatic Stress: the Effects of Overwhelming Experience on Mind, Body and Society*. London: Guilford Press.

Vasterman, Peter, C. Joris Yzermans, and Anja J.E. Dirkzwager. 2005a. The Role of the Media and Media Hypes in the Aftermath of Disasters. *Epidemiology Review* 27: 112–124.

Vasterman, Peter, C. Joris Yzermans, and Anja J.E. Dirkzwager. 2005b. The Role of the Media and Media Hypes in the Aftermath of Disasters. *Journal of Traumatic Stress* 19: 639–651.

Videka-Sherman, Lynn. 1982. Coping with the Death of a Child: A Study Over Time. *American Journal of Orthopsychiatry* 52(4): 688–698.

Walter, Tony. 1996. A New Model of Grief: Bereavement and Biography. *Mortality: Promoting the Interdisciplinary Study of Death and Dying* 1(1): 7–25.

Walther, Sarah. 2010. *Interview with Sarah Walther*. DISPUK Seminar, Crete.

West, Wendy R. 2005. Some Early Impressions in the Aftermath of Hurricane Katrina. *International Journal of Narrative Therapy and Community Work* 3&4: 5–9.

White, Michael. 1984. Pseudo-Encropresis: From Avalanche to Victory, from Vicious to Virtuous Cycles." *Family Systems Medicine* 2(2): xx–xx.

—. 1985. Fear Busting and Monster Training. *Dulwich Centre Review* 29-34.: http://www.narrativetherapylibrary.com/fear-busting-and-monster-taming-an-approach-to-the-fears-of-young-children.html

—. 1999. *Re-engaging with History: the Absent but Implicit.* The Narrative Therapy and Community Work Conference. February 1999, Adelaide.

—. 2000. Reflecting Teamwork as Definitional Ceremony Re-Visited. In Reflections on Narrative Practice: Essays and Interviews, edited by Michael White. Adelaide: Dulwich Publications.

—. 2003. Narrative Practice and Community Assignments. *International Journal of Narrative Therapy and Community Work* 2: 31-37.

—. 2005. Workshop Notes. *Statements of Positions Map: 5-9: http://www.narrativetherapylibrary.com/media/downloadable/files/links/m/i/michael-white-workshop-notes_2.pdf*

—. 2006. Working with People who are Suffering from the Consequences of Multiple Trauma: A Narrative Perspective. In *Trauma: Narrative Responses to Traumatic Events*, edited by David Denborough. Adelaide: Dulwich Centre Publications 25–85.

—. 2007a. *Maps of Narrative Practice.* London: W.W. Norton and Company Ltd.

—. 2007b. Working with Trauma. International Conference of Narrative Therapy and Community Work, Norway, June 2007.

White, Michael, and David Epston. 1990. *Narrative Means to Therapeutic Ends*. New York: W.W. Norton and Company.

INDEX OF CONTRIBUTORS